WHAT TO SAY
WHEN 2
YOUR PROVEN GUIDE IN THE
NEW ABORTION LANDSCAPE

Also by Shawn Carney

*40 Days for Life: Discover What God Has Done . . .
Imagine What He Can Do* (2013)

*The Beginning of the End of Abortion: 40 Inspiring
Stories of God Changing Hearts and Saving Lives*
(2018)

*To the Heart of the Matter: The 40-Day Companion
to Live a Culture of Life* (2020)

*What to Say When: The Complete New Guide
to Discussing Abortion* (2021)

Also by Steve Karlen

*This Is When We Begin to Fight: A Family's
Battle Against Late-Term Abortion, Academia . . .
and Miscarriage at Home* (2019)

*What to Say When: The Complete New Guide
to Discussing Abortion* (2021)

WHAT TO SAY
WHEN 2

YOUR PROVEN GUIDE IN THE
NEW ABORTION LANDSCAPE

How to Discuss, Clarify, and Question
Abortion in a Hostile Culture

SHAWN D. CARNEY
AND
STEVE KARLEN

K|A
KOLBE & ANTHONY
PUBLISHING

ISBN: 978-1-7370477-8-0

Cover design: Jam Graphic Design
Interior layout and e-book: LParnell Book Services

Printed in the United States of America

31 30 29 28 27 26 25 24   1 2 3 4 5

*For the selfless men and women who have served
this great cause longer than we have been alive—
and for those who are no longer with us.*

Contents

The monstrous injustice of slavery . . .
deprives our republican example of its just influence
in the world—enables the enemies of free institutions,
with plausibility, to taunt us as hypocrites.

— Abraham Lincoln, 1854[1]

❧ ❧ ❧

High Tide

Success waits patiently for anyone who has
the determination and strength to seize it.
— Booker T. Washington[1]

The sand dunes at the beaches in Galveston, Texas, are infested with venomous western diamondback rattlesnakes. Warning signs for beachgoers everywhere go ignored.

I (Shawn) ignore them, too, as I drag our cooler, umbrellas, fishing poles, chairs, toys, and endless snacks through the dunes for a family day at the beach. I look ridiculous, but if I get everything to our spot overlooking the Gulf of Mexico in a single trip, it's one less trek through the rattlesnakes.

Sweat beads on my face as I finish setting everything up. I sit in my chair, grab my coffee, and take in the breathtaking view of the morning sun glistening on the water. The tide is high this morning. The crowds haven't yet arrived, and I lose myself in the serenity of the surf and seagulls as I wait for my wife, Marilisa, and eight kids to join me.

At first the tranquility of it all keeps me from noticing my bride running toward my chair shouting over and over again, "They did it! They did it! They did it!"

"They" were the Supreme Court of the United States, and "it" was the overturning of *Roe v. Wade*.

That's where I was, calmly admiring the Gulf of Mexico on June 24, 2022, when the Supreme Court corrected a 50-year error that an all-male Supreme Court imposed upon us in 1973.

Where were you?

Remember where you were, what you were doing, thinking, and feeling, and share it with your friends, kids, grandchildren, and great-grandchildren. Moments like this don't come along often, and many pro-life heroes didn't live to experience that glorious day.

An hour later I was on the BBC, and the rest of the day was a wild but exhilarating whirlwind. The days, months, and years to follow promise to be no different.

In the coming pages, we will distinguish facts from fiction and fantasy from reality in the new landscape of a post-*Roe* America. The point is—as we said in the first *What to Say When* book—not to be a know-it-all who can stick it to people when abortion comes up in daily conversation. If that is your goal, this book will help you, no doubt. But it will only help your mind and your ego and do nothing for the hearts and souls with whom you engage, much less your own heart and soul. Hearts and souls are the end goal because it is hearts and souls that got us into the crisis of 73 million lives lost to abortion globally each year.[2] And hearts and souls are what will navigate our country and world to be abortion-free.

The historic overturning of *Roe v. Wade* was a beautiful interruption to our family vacation and a great awakening that shocked the world. *You* are needed in this shocked world. You cannot be an observer because we need you. We need you to bring clarity, we need you to bring science, we need you to bring reason, we need you to bring joy, and above all we need you to bring love.

Love is the solution to the anger, pain, and despair that abortion thrives on. It's high tide for saving lives and ending abortion—and there's much work to be done.

The Heart Is the Key to the Mind

As we enter this book, know that this epic battle for life is ultimately won on our knees. Our prayers and fasting are our most powerful resources in this struggle.

Yes, it's true you don't need to believe in God to be against abortion. Any reasonable person should be against abortion. Many atheists and agnostics are pro-life. The intellectual case for abortion is easy to refute, and the beautiful biological realities of life are easy to embrace.

But the abortion crisis goes much deeper than a debate over biology. Many things must go wrong for a woman to feel she has no other choice than to pay a healer to violently end the life of her baby. Even more must go wrong for that doctor to agree to do it and for the state to approve of it and even to help pay for it.

This is a spiritual battle that forces us to ask, and answer, the most basic and essential questions of human life: What is it? Where does it come from? And why is it sacred?

Abortion survives not because its supporters make a strong intellectual case but because pain, confusion, and sometimes anger fuel a relentless push to keep it legal. When discussing abortion, that's why the tone we use is critical.

We don't know a single former abortion worker who was 100 percent pro-life when she walked out of her job. But after leaving their jobs, former workers' hearts were touched by the Christian charity they witnessed in pro-life prayer warriors. Love softens hearts and leads even the staunchest abortion supporters to the realization that life in the womb is real, inherently precious, and deserving of protection.

The overturning of *Roe v. Wade* was one of the greatest days in American history. As a result, the stakes have never been higher. Let us guard our hearts, sharpen our minds, and proceed with love as we speak for the voiceless and navigate our way through the rattlesnakes. Let's get started!

CHAPTER 1

Who Was and Wasn't Ready?

To live is to change, and to be perfect is to have changed often.
— St. John Henry Newman[1]

In our divided culture, we all agree on one ancient teaching: original sin. No matter what side of any issue you're on, we all agree that we are not as we ought to be. What gives us hope, both individual and societal, is the possibility of change. People can change, nations can change, and cultures can change. We can change for the worse or the better, but change is always possible with human hearts and souls. Change gives us hope that things can get better and fear that they may get worse. When change arrives, whether we are for it or against it, it can shock us.

Who Was Ready?

The Grassroots

For over 50 years, pregnancy resource centers have not waited for Washington, DC, to correct the moral crisis in their own backyard. They went to work at the most important level in America—the grassroots—building more than 3,000 pregnancy resource centers[2] that now outnumber abortion providers more than 4 to 1[3] in the United States. This ratio continues to increase every year.[4]

Decade after decade, not only were more pregnancy centers being built, but those pregnancy centers were also growing more sophisticated, professionalizing, and expanding the number and availability of the free services they offer women. Many pro-life pregnancy centers do all of this without government funding, making them beautiful examples of communities helping those in need.

Today, your average pregnancy center offers free pregnancy tests, free sexually transmitted disease tests, free ultrasounds, and free prenatal care from a registered nurse or medical doctor. You will only see a doctor at Planned Parenthood if you are going to have an abortion. Contrary to the myth that abortion is between a woman and her doctor, former (and a few current) abortionists will testify they are not an abortion client's personal doctor. They have never seen their abortion clients before. They usually don't know their names. And they often don't want the women getting abortions knowing their names.

The effectiveness, professionalism, and independent nature of pregnancy resource centers are disastrous for the bottom line of abortion facilities—especially when a pregnancy resource center is near an abortion facility, which has become increasingly common during the past 20 years. The proliferation of pregnancy resource centers did not happen overnight. It's the fruit of the pro-life movement going to work year after year on *hearts and minds* no matter what the Supreme Court did or what the political environment looked like.

Now add a million 40 Days for Life participants peacefully praying outside their local abortion facilities in 1,700 locations and referring women to pregnancy centers, and you have a robust local pro-life movement. 40 Days for Life is built for post-*Roe* America, which is why prior to the fall of *Roe*, 45 percent of all the abortion facilities that closed during or following one of our internationally coordinated 40-day peaceful vigils were located in blue, pro-abortion states, where abortion remains legal and even celebrated.

America's largest collections of 40 Days for Life vigils are found in the most pro-abortion states. California has led the way since 2008. This is significant in a post-*Roe* America, especially when momentum and morale for local abortion facilities have hit all-time lows.

State Legislators

One of the many reasons the Supreme Court overturned *Roe* was because *Roe* prevented states from regulating abortion. That lack of regulation meant an invasive surgery was less regulated than a haircut or a manicure. The abortion industry was the Wild West.

State after state tried to enact reforms—including by mandating basic health and safety regulations for abortion facilities. And state after state saw their efforts to protect women from an unregulated abortion industry hit a brick wall in *Roe*. A steady stream of lawsuits over abortion facility regulations wore down the Supreme Court and no doubt played a role in the court deciding that abortion law should go back to the states.

Those lawsuits also led pro-life states to take proactive action anticipating the day when *Roe* would no longer serve as a *de facto* protection racket for the abortion industry. Those states prepared for the fall of *Roe* by enacting "trigger laws," which would regulate abortion—or prohibit it altogether—once *Roe* was overturned. Thirteen states enacted trigger laws. Once *Roe* fell, these states essentially became abortion-free, earning their place in history among the first wave of states to protect unborn children from abortion:

- Arkansas
- Idaho
- Kentucky
- Louisiana
- Mississippi
- Missouri
- North Dakota
- Oklahoma
- South Dakota
- Tennessee
- Texas
- Utah
- Wyoming[5]

These 13 states wrapped themselves in glory, but they take second place to Alabama, which had already protected life from conception years before the overturning of *Roe*.[6] Alabama's law took effect after that overturning. *Roll Tide!*

As of the writing of this book, the number of states protecting human life has swelled to 22—nearly half of the country.[7]

Who Was Not Ready?

Abortion Activists

When an angry toddler tosses a gallon of milk out of a shopping cart in response to some perceived injustice committed by his big sister, it's mom and dad's job to remind the child that it's not acceptable to throw a temper tantrum. "Use your words," parents teach their children—at least if they want their kids to grow up to be well-adjusted adults. Mature adults communicate their frustrations rather than resorting to violence.

The post-*Roe* world made it clear that abortion supporters never learned this lesson. When the Supreme Court announced the *Dobbs v. Jackson Women's Health Organization* ruling, pro-choicers didn't write a pro-abortion version of *What to Say When.* Like the toddler at the grocery store, they broke things.

And ironically, at the top of their list of targets were pregnancy help centers that offer free medical and material help to women and families facing challenging pregnancies. By day, abortion advocates appeared in the media and demanded that pro-lifers explain how we intended to support every woman denied access to abortion by the *Dobbs* decision. By night, they firebombed the clinics that provide that very support.

We've spoken at hundreds of fundraising events for pregnancy help centers. Almost every time, we meet an abortion advocate who introduces himself after our talk, shares what he agreed and disagreed with, and concludes, "But we can all agree we're fortunate to have this pregnancy center in our community, and it's worthy of our support."

Even in the minds of abortion supporters, pregnancy centers are the *good guys* in the pro-life movement!

We understand why people don't like pro-life marches, lobbyists, and those of us who stand on the sidewalk as activists. We've been heckled, yelled at, and spat on. We get it; some people don't like public opposition to abortion. But firebombing pregnancy centers offering free help to women is the last thing we predicted from abortion supporters after the fall of *Roe.*

It's also a good sign for pro-lifers. Abortion supporters threw a temper tantrum precisely because it's the *only* thing they were prepared to do.

The Media

It's clear that the media really didn't think *Roe* would *ever* be overturned.

It's not just that they were upset about it, which was expected. It's that mainstream media personalities could not—or would not—understand the Supreme Court's legal and intellectual reasons for reversing *Roe*. No one on television seems even to have read the opinion. They were too busy eating their own, condemning Democrats who didn't vote for Hillary Clinton in 2016 because they were faithful to Bernie Sanders and trashing the late Supreme Court Justice Ruth Bader Ginsburg.

It's easy to understand the media personalities' rage against Democrats who refused to pull the lever for Hillary. Perhaps with better voter turnout, she would have won the White House, preventing Donald Trump from appointing three justices instrumental to the *Dobbs* decision. But why turn on their own Ruth Bader Ginsburg, whom they made into a folk hero, *the Notorious RBG*? For decades, she was the epitome of the feminist, pro-abortion movement. Her former boosters, however, despised her after the fall of *Roe* for two reasons:

1. She didn't resign under President Obama and then died during Trump's presidency, allowing Trump to replace her with pro-life Justice Amy Coney Barrett.
2. She was intellectually honest enough to criticize *Roe* publicly (more on this in a later chapter).

It wasn't rational for pro-abortion talking heads to throw their longtime idol under the bus after she died. But people usually become irrational when they're unprepared for a shock to their world.

Republicans

The news isn't all good for pro-lifers. The backlash to the overturning of *Roe* brought about the greatest expansion and radicalization of abortion laws since *Roe* itself. It's not so much that the abortion industry was ready for the overturning of *Roe* as that supposedly pro-life Republican politicians weren't ready to make their case against the barbarity of abortion.

For decades, Republicans have enjoyed the support of pro-life voters. And in many cases, pro-lifers enjoyed the fruit of Republican victories:

- At the state level, Republicans made great progress regulating abortion and defunding Planned Parenthood.
- At the federal level, Republicans confirmed the Supreme Court justices who finally overturned *Roe*.

Many politicians accomplished pro-life policy objectives, but with few exceptions, they did so without ever having to discuss what abortion is. The lack of experience articulating a coherent pro-life platform now shows, as Republicans appear lost, scared, or ignorant when abortion comes up on the campaign trail or in a debate hall. They, too, act as though they never expected *Roe* to go away. Now that it has, they're too paralyzed by fear of the political fallout to make the case for life.

Democrats

Republicans aren't the only politicians who got lazy because *Roe v. Wade* created abortion legislation gridlock for five decades. As long as Democrats could parrot the talking point that they support the precedent of *Roe*, they could count on abortion supporters' votes. They, too, were ill equipped to discuss abortion beyond the surface level. For the first time, they must now confront the realities of unborn babies' heartbeats, fetal development, abortion survivors, and biology in general.

They've refused to do so. Instead, they simply declared the Supreme Court "illegitimate," demanded taxpayer-funded abortion up to 40 weeks (or beyond), and denied health care to babies who survive abortion. Few Democrats voiced such radical positions prior to the Trump administration and the overturning of *Roe*. It's now the norm within the party.

Planned Parenthood

As the nation's largest abortion provider, Planned Parenthood responded to the reversal of *Roe* by mobilizing its supporters to . . . host gatherings in their homes to share why they support abortion rights.[8] That was it. Their X (formerly Twitter) feed highlighted Pride Month, transgender rights, and gun laws.

Planned Parenthood's response to an existential threat was pathetic, as it repeatedly strayed off mission. The *Titanic* had hit the iceberg, but the abortion giant's weakest (and wokest) CEO in decades was too distracted by the latest diversity, equity, and inclusion flavor of the week to scramble the lifeboats.

Weird Is the New Normal

You don't need a book to tell you that things got *weird* after the overturning of *Roe*. But we can navigate weird by sticking to the basics whenever abortion or the fall of *Roe* come up in conversation.

Remember two things:

1. Almost no one has read Justice Samuel Alito's opinion overturning *Roe*.
2. The only other example we have of the Supreme Court dehumanizing an entire segment of our population is slavery.

It's generally assumed that the first one in a discussion to bring up slavery or Nazis loses the debate. But in America, slavery is the only *appropriate* comparison to abortion because we've dehumanized a segment of our population only one other time until *Roe* came along. It's all we have.

When *Roe* comes up, ask questions. People rarely want to listen to your opinions, or even your facts. But they love to share their own. By asking the right questions, you might just guide an abortion advocate to persuade *himself* that abortion should join *Roe* on the scrap heap of history.

Questions to Ask Abortion Supporters

You: *Why did the Supreme Court overturn* Roe?

Them: They are bigoted activists who hate women and want us to go back to patriarchy. They even want women to birth their rapists' babies. The Supreme Court should be dismantled.

You: *That would be alarming, but those aren't the reasons given in the legal opinion. What was inaccurate in the legal opinion that overturned* Roe?

Them: *Roe* was a well-established precedent, and the court took away 50 years of basic human rights guaranteed by the Constitution. Women are no longer free to control their own bodies. The Supreme Court declared women to be subhuman.

You: *The only historical reference we have as Americans is the last time the Supreme Court dehumanized a segment of our population that many Americans viewed as subhuman. The decision was* Dred Scott, *which declared enslaved persons to be the property of the slave owners. Leading up to the Civil War, we had free states and slave states. Do you agree we are headed in that direction again with states where abortion is legal and states where it's illegal?*

Them: Yes. For sure, the Supreme Court is treating women like slaves.

You: *Alabama banned abortion[9] based on the biological reality that life starts at conception and therefore deserves protection. New York expanded abortion through all 40 weeks of pregnancy,[10] does not require a licensed physician to do the abortion,[11] and will not provide medical assistance to a baby who survives an abortion.[12] Do you think New York or Alabama is the free state in this situation?*

Them: Alabama is not free because it enslaves women by denying them access to abortion. New York is empowering women by expanding their reproductive rights.

You: *So before abortion was legalized in 1973, would you have considered every state in America to be a slave state?*

Them: Maybe, in a way.

You: *When Congress passed the Thirteenth Amendment ending slavery, was that an infringement on the rights of plantation owners who depended on slaves to provide for the well-being of their families and community? Wasn't, in fact, the government overreaching in order to deprive them of providing for their families and control over their private property?*

Them: No, that's crazy. Slavery needed to be corrected. *Roe* didn't need correction and was a 50-year legal precedent.

You: *Was the Emancipation Proclamation, which freed the slaves, a violation of the well-established legal and constitutional precedent of* Dred Scott?

Them: No, because slavery should have been declared unconstitutional. The *Dred Scott* decision got it wrong.

You: *The Supreme Court overturned* Roe *for the same reason the* Dred Scott *decision is a black eye on our nation to this day:* Roe *was unconstitutional.*

CHAPTER 2

Roe v. Wade Was Never Viable

We therefore hold that the Constitution does not confer a right to abortion. Roe *and* Casey *must be overruled, and the authority to regulate abortion must be returned to the people and their elected representatives.*

—Dobbs v. Jackson Women's Health Organization[1]

For nearly five decades, *Roe v. Wade* was the abortion industry's ultimate cheat code, preventing Americans from protecting unborn babies at the federal, state, and local levels. But the same ruling that allowed abortion businesses to kill more than 63 million babies in the womb over a five-decade span[2] also became something of an Achilles' heel for the industry because it made abortion advocates *lazy*.

Abortion supporters quit making the case for abortion. With *Roe* in place, there was no need to win hearts or minds—not when even basic common-sense health and safety regulations of abortion facilities would be hastily struck down by the federal judiciary as "undue burdens" on a woman's "right to choose."

It's hard to blame abortion advocates for their reluctance to defend abortion. After all, when people talk about abortion, they learn about abortion. And when people learn about abortion, they just might find out what abortion looks like,

17

what abortion feels like, what abortion sounds like, what abortion *smells* like.

When people talk about abortion, they might learn about the women tormented by nightmares decades after their abortions. Or the babies who survived their abortion appointments—only to be abandoned in a utility closet or disposed of in a bucket of formaldehyde.[3] They might find out how abortions are performed. They might discover the disturbing connections between abortion and human sex trafficking.[4]

Talking about abortion is *dangerous* for abortion supporters. It's much safer—much more expedient—to talk about *Roe*. Because as long as the abortion industry had *Roe*, it was free to continue aborting a million babies a year. Unwilling to discuss the merits of abortion, abortion advocates steered many an abortion conversation to *Roe*.

"*Roe v. Wade* is settled law."

"It's the law of the land."

"Reversing *Roe* would be the first time the Supreme Court ever took away a constitutional right."

"*Roe* is sacrosanct."

Indeed, every religion has its sacred text, and the abortion lobby's was the *Roe* decision. Devotees to the mantra that *Roe* was "binding precedent" even managed to persuade Supreme Court Chief Justice John Roberts to abandon his pro-life convictions, or at least to subject those pro-life convictions to another quasireligious belief: the infallibility of the nation's high court.

Their overreliance on *Roe* explains abortion supporters' pearl-clutching at the mere suggestion that *Roe* might one day be overturned. It explains the moral panic that ensued when *Politico* published a leaked draft opinion indicating the Supreme Court would reverse *Roe*.[5] And it explains the violent attacks on churches, faith-based pregnancy help centers, and pro-life organizations' offices when *Roe* finally was overturned.

But lost amidst the fiery rhetoric and the firebombed pregnancy centers is an uncomfortable reality the abortion industry would rather not consider: *Roe v. Wade* was always destined for the scrap heap.

It wasn't inevitable that *Roe* would give way to a pro-life ruling like the *Dobbs v. Jackson Women's Health Organization* decision. The Supreme Court could have used some other rationale to reaffirm the legality of abortion—or even to expand it. But the court's vacuous reasoning made *Roe* a lame duck from the beginning. One way or another, it was only a matter of time before it would be shelved.

Remember these three points whenever it's suggested that *Roe* was settled law that never should have been revisited.

Point 1: *Roe v. Wade* Was Doomed from the Start

The obvious problem with the Supreme Court declaring a constitutional right to abortion is that the Constitution doesn't actually say *anything* about abortion. "The Constitution has no more to say about abortion than it does quantum physics," wrote former National Review Institute fellow Kevin Williamson. "And the Founding Fathers knew where babies come from—if they had wanted to put something in the national charter relating to pregnancy, they could have done so."[6]

Veteran *Los Angeles Times* Supreme Court and legal writer David G. Savage noted that in crafting the *Roe* ruling, Justice Harry Blackmun surveyed centuries' worth of abortion opinions held by Persians, Greeks, Romans, and the English. "He did not, however, quote a provision in the Constitution that protected abortion rights."[7]

With no right to abortion to be found in the Constitution or in America's history and tradition, abortion supporters argued that laws protecting unborn children violated the constitutional right to "personal privacy" and "privacy in the doctor-patient relationship."[8] One might wonder: If a right to privacy trumps protection of the innocent from violence, what prevents the high court from striking down laws on domestic battery or child abuse—provided that the beatings take place behind closed doors in the privacy of one's own home?

Asserting a constitutional right to privacy appears to be an odd strategy given that the Constitution doesn't mention privacy any more than it mentions abortion or quantum physics. "The Constitution does not explicitly mention any right of privacy," Blackmun wrote on behalf of the majority. Nevertheless, Blackmun went on to justify legalizing abortion nationwide based on . . . a constitutional right to privacy.[9]

In overturning *Roe*, Justice Samuel Alito and the *Dobbs* majority acknowledged that Blackmun's justification was highly speculative. "[*Roe's*] message seemed to be that the abortion right could be found somewhere in the Constitution and that specifying its exact location was not of paramount importance."[10]

But the Supreme Court's willingness to make up new rights to abortion and to privacy out of whole cloth isn't the only reason *Roe* was doomed from the start. The ruling also dismissed the abortion debate's central controversy as irrelevant. "We need not resolve the difficult question of when life begins," Blackmun wrote.[11]

Really? The question of when life begins is *the entire debate*. If the fetus is not a living human being, nobody would oppose abortion, and Texas wouldn't have had an abortion ban on the books for *Roe* to strike down. But if the fetus is a living human being, the case in favor of abortion requires you to declare that some human beings are unworthy of even the most basic human rights—a position most people don't want to take (at least publicly). Even if the fetus "could be" a human being, abortion would be wrong. Firemen don't wait on the front lawn of a burning house where there "could be" children inside. We don't drive kids in our car knowing they "could be" unbuckled, nor do we run over a raccoon if we think it "could be" a two-year-old.

Of course, Blackmun's assertion that the question of when life begins is "difficult" was scientifically illiterate at best. The embryo, zygote, or whatever stage of development you want to use carries out biological processes like growth, nutrition, and before long, movement and response to stimuli, making it clear that life is present. And the presence of a distinct human genome makes it clear that this life in the womb is *human* life. Since *Roe* was decided, advancements in embryology and ultrasound technology have only made it clearer that human life begins at fertilization.

And speaking of scientific advancement, medical breakthroughs saving the lives of babies born earlier and earlier in pregnancy put a final nail in the coffin of *Roe*. Both *Roe* and its successor, *Planned Parenthood v. Casey*,[12] affirmed a right to abortion before fetal viability—that is, before the unborn child is capable of surviving outside the womb. But this viability standard is exceptionally arbitrary. Is there a precise *moment* when the unborn child becomes viable? And is the moment the same for all unborn children? Blackmun didn't seem to think so. "Viability is usually placed at about seven months (28 weeks) but may occur earlier, even at 24 weeks," he wrote.[13]

What? Based on what science? His legal opinion that day?

Years later, the viability police would say 23 weeks, then 22 weeks. If living outside the womb on your own without your mom is the standard for personhood, many adults today would be in danger of being dehumanized. Viability can be very relative.

The point of viability continues to change. On July 5, 2020, Curtis and C'Asya Means were born at just 21 weeks and a day. Tragically, C'Asya didn't survive. But when Curtis left the hospital six months later, Guinness World Records recognized him as the most premature baby ever to survive.[14] That puts viability three to seven weeks earlier than Justice Blackmun calculated in 1973. Perhaps by the time you read this book, another little girl or boy will have broken Curtis's record.

In any case, as medical technology changes the viability timeline, it grows increasingly difficult to suggest that viability determines whether a child has a right to life. Did every abortion-vulnerable 22-week-old baby suddenly gain human rights when Baby Curtis survived his premature birth? "We've had this very blurred line when it came to viability," said Mississippi Attorney General Lynn Fitch, who filed the *Dobbs* case. "Every court had a different opinion [about when a fetus becomes viable]. . . . *Roe* never gave clear direction. . . . How do you know which one you follow?"[15]

With no definitive answer, *Roe* would need to be fixed, if for no other reason than to address the logistical problems. But even if viability could be pinned down to the second, what sort of existential transformation takes place in that moment that suddenly endows the unborn child with fundamental human rights? Blackmun offered no answers.

The viability standard isn't just arbitrary; it's *mean*. Civilized society prioritizes the protection of its most vulnerable members. This is why we have laws that protect children, racial and religious minorities, and people with disabilities. We pay taxes to fund programs that provide a safety net to those who need one. But the viability standard established in *Roe* and *Casey* reverses our instinct toward compassion by discriminating against the children *most* in need of protection.

Point 2: Even Abortion Supporters Recognized That *Roe* Was a Train Wreck

It's not just pro-lifers who note that *Roe* was a shoddy ruling. Justice Sandra Day O'Connor, who later reaffirmed the central holding of *Roe* in *Casey*, realized early on that *Roe*'s reasoning was ridiculous. "The *Roe* framework, then, is clearly on a collision course with itself," O'Connor wrote in her dissent in an abortion case a decade after *Roe*. "As medical science becomes better able to provide for the separate existence of the fetus, the point of viability is moved further back toward conception."[16]

Harvard legal scholar John Hart Ely—who supported legal abortion—was even harsher in his assessment of *Roe*'s merits. "*Roe* is bad because it is bad constitutional law, or rather because it is not constitutional law and gives almost no sense of an obligation to try to be."[17]

Ouch.

Blackmun's own law clerk and dear friend Edward Lazarus agreed: "As a matter of constitutional interpretation and judicial method, *Roe* borders on the indefensible. I say this as someone utterly committed to the right to choose, as someone who loved *Roe*'s author like a grandfather."[18]

Double ouch.

Even Supreme Court justice and pro-abortion icon Ruth Bader Ginsburg had sharp criticism for the decision. "The court wrote a sweeping opinion that made every law in the country, even the most liberal, unconstitutional," she said in a 2016 interview. The Notorious RBG described the ruling as "going too far too fast" and critiqued its emphasis on "privacy."[19] Make no mistake: Ginsburg supported legal abortion through and through. But she did have the intellectual honesty to recognize that *Roe*'s justification for striking down 50 states' worth of abortion laws was flawed from the start.

Perhaps most telling is, when *Dobbs* overturned *Roe*, not even the dissenting justices made a credible attempt to defend *Roe*'s legal reasoning. Associate Justices Stephen Breyer, Sonia Sotomayor, and Elena Kagan just regurgitated a long litany of tired talking points you'd expect to hear at a Planned Parenthood rally. There's rhetoric about forced birth, the importance of aborting babies with disabilities, and women needing to kill children in order to achieve equality with men. The dissent spent pages discussing the supposed rights to same-sex marriage and contraception as well as perceived negative implications the justices believe will follow the overturning of *Roe*. Apparently lacking any sense of irony, the dissent lamented the supposed loss of a constitutional right: "Throughout our history, the sphere of protected liberty has expanded, bringing in individuals formerly excluded."[20] There's even a reference to the tabletop game Jenga.[21]

But, like *Roe*, the dissent never found the part of the Constitution that establishes a right to kill a child.

Point 3: Overturning *Roe* Is a Generational Step Forward for Empowering Women

"It's a brand-new day for America!" declared Mississippi Attorney General Lynn Fitch the Monday after she won the case that overturned *Roe*. "What a victory for the women

[and] children! . . . It truly spoke to the empowerment of women and protecting life."[22] Fitch's remarks stood in stark contrast to those of abortion supporters cosplaying in *The Handmaid's Tale* outfits and shouting, "We won't go back!" But there's nothing progressive about pitting mothers against their babies. Real progress means empowering both, which makes the overturning of *Roe* a monumental step forward for women.

The argument for upholding *Roe* was even more radical than *Roe* itself—and in a thoroughly misogynistic way. The first paragraph of the *Dobbs* dissent declared, "Respecting a woman as an autonomous being, and granting her full equality, meant giving her substantial choice over this most personal and most consequential of all life decisions."[23]

In other words, without the ability to kill their children, women can never be equal to men. And if you're a woman who is pro-life, your opinion on the matter is irrelevant.

What could be more demeaning to women than to suggest they are defective *unless* they wield the power to destroy that most beautiful and awesome genius—their unique ability to conceive, bear, nourish, and nurture a new human being?

The *Dobbs* dissenters go so far as to claim that women define themselves by their ability to destroy the life they bear. "The expectation of reproductive control is integral to many women's identity . . . ," the justices wrote. "That expectation helps define a woman as an 'equal citizen,' with all the rights, privileges, and obligations that status entails."[24]

This sort of rhetoric plays well in the university faculty lounge, where abortion can be discussed abstractly. Not so much when one considers what abortion actually is and what it does. To insist that a woman's dignity depends on crushed skulls and severed limbs is a cruel and grim way to define femininity. And it's a striking contrast with Cardinal Joseph Mindszenty's praise for motherhood:

> The most important person on earth is a mother. She cannot claim the honor of having built Notre Dame Cathedral. She need not. She has built something more magnificent than any cathedral—a dwelling for an immortal soul, the tiny perfection of her baby's body. . . . The angels have not been blessed with such a grace. They cannot share in God's creative miracle to bring new saints to Heaven. Only a human mother can. Mothers are closer to God the Creator than any other creature; God joins forces with mothers in performing this act of creation. . . . What on God's good earth is more glorious than this: to be a mother?[25]

Real empowerment doesn't force a woman to choose between killing her dreams and killing her child. It equips her to have both. "Fifty years ago, for professional women, they wanted you to make a choice," Fitch said. "Now you don't have to. Now you have the opportunity to be whatever you want to be. You have the option in life to really achieve your dreams, your goals, and you can have those beautiful children as well."[26]

Making abortion the default response to a crisis pregnancy disincentivizes finding solutions. "They offer no . . . positive direction for the women," Fitch said.[27] Governments and employers would rather help a woman terminate her pregnancy than her crisis. But when abortion is off the table, it forces society to do what pro-life Christians have been doing for decades: roll up our sleeves and support moms in need. Fitch has pushed initiatives in Mississippi to increase support for mothers in crisis, and she's not alone among pro-life public officials.

But when abortion ended in Mississippi, so too did the abortion industry's interest in Mississippi women. Rather than working to support expectant moms in the post-*Roe* era, Jackson Women's Health Organization abandoned the state. Today there are more than 30 pregnancy resource centers offering free medical and material help to women.[28] Abortion advocates had no interest in this and left the state the day after *Roe* fell. This beautiful reality highlights how *Roe* bred laziness and dependency, while the pro-life movement went to work to change hearts and minds and offer tangible alternatives. It's a sign of a movement built to last.

What to Say When Abortion Supporters Say *Roe V. Wade* Was Settled Law:

- *Roe* was created out of thin air and doomed from the start.
- Even abortion supporters recognized *Roe* was bad law and unconstitutional.
- Overturning *Roe* was legal common sense that was inevitable because of scientific advancements.

CHAPTER 3

Deer in the Headlights: Five New Pro-Abortion Myths

Repeating the big lie often enough convinces the public.

—Dr. Bernard Nathanson, founder of NARAL,
former abortion provider[1]

The world spent June 2022 watching and waiting for the Supreme Court to overturn *Roe v. Wade*. But you wouldn't have known it from following Planned Parenthood's Twitter (now X) feed.

It's not like the abortion giant didn't have time to get ready. The nation's high court agreed to take the *Dobbs v. Jackson Women's Health Organization* case more than a year earlier.[2] The Supreme Court heard oral arguments on December 1, 2021. And by early May, *Politico* had published a leaked draft decision indicating the court would overturn *Roe*.[3]

Planned Parenthood only managed to keep its eye on the ball for a couple of weeks. The organization held nationally coordinated "Bans Off Our Bodies" rallies on May 14 with a website and a social media hashtag to go with it.[4] But by the end of the month, references to *Roe* and the Supreme Court all but vanished.

With the court poised to throw Planned Parenthood into a fight for its very survival, the abortion empire barely posted about *Roe*. It did, however, have a lot to say about all kinds of other supposed social justice issues that aren't exactly central to the abortion chain's core product:

- Salaries for the U.S. Women's National Soccer Team players
- Immigrant Heritage Month
- A "safe space playlist"
- Juneteenth
- Gun violence
- Ending the "stigma" of sexually transmitted infections[5] (featuring a link to an article that describes how to reduce one's risk of contracting HIV while sleeping with or sharing needles with someone who is HIV positive)[6]

Planned Parenthood tweeted about abortion, too, but those posts didn't exactly convey the urgency of the moment. There was little evidence of any sort of a coordinated campaign to respond to the imminent reversal of *Roe*. Once the calendar turned to June, the "#BansOffOurBodies" hashtag disappeared entirely until June 23[7]—the day before *Roe* fell. By all appearances, Planned Parenthood's social media staffer went on a three-week vacation and lazily auto-scheduled tweets highlighting an assortment of flavor-of-the-week progressive causes.

But Planned Parenthood's social-justice-cause-du-jour approach to the most fraught month in its history wasn't merely the work of an incompetent social media director. The Twitter/X debacle was just one symptom of an existential crisis years in the making.

Longtime Planned Parenthood president and CEO Cecile Richards announced her resignation in January 2018.[8] Throughout her dozen years at the helm, Richards built Planned Parenthood into a political heavyweight. Her presidency saw the organization more than quadruple its volunteer and supporter base.[9] Richards successfully prevented Congress from defunding Planned Parenthood. And she helped Planned Parenthood escape largely unscathed throughout David Daleiden's 2015 undercover exposé revealing that Planned Parenthood had been trafficking body parts harvested from aborted babies.

Richards's departure was a big blow to Planned Parenthood, and one that appeared to catch the abortion business by surprise, as it took eight months to name Dr. Leana Wen as her successor.[10] While Richards—the daughter of former Texas governor Ann Richards—made her name in the political world, Wen was chosen to highlight Planned Parenthood not just as an activist organization but as a medical institution.[11]

It didn't take long for buyer's remorse to set in. Hiring a young, technocratic physician sounded good on paper. But Wen's approach to running Planned Parenthood wasn't a good fit for an organization rooted in radical politics. "The emergency physician and former Baltimore health commissioner had tried to position the organization as a nonpartisan healthcare institution, but its board wanted to double down on its progressive, pro-abortion advocacy," wrote Anna Medaris in *Business Insider*.[12]

The friction led to Wen's ouster after less than a year on the job.[13] "I wanted to emphasize total women's health," Wen recounted. "They wanted to double down on abortion rights."[14]

Planned Parenthood tapped former board member Alexis McGill Johnson as acting president and CEO[15] and—nearly a year after announcing a search for a permanent president—removed the "acting" tag in June 2020.[16] There was no danger of McGill Johnson being insufficiently zealous when it came to pitching abortion. A retread who served as Planned Parenthood's board chair, PAC chair, and Planned Parenthood Action Fund board member, McGill Johnson is "a long-standing champion for social and racial justice, a respected political and cultural organizer, and a tireless advocate for reproductive freedom" according to her official biography.[17]

Be careful what you wish for.

McGill Johnson's call for a more "intersectional"[18] pro-abortion movement explains the mission drift that led Planned Parenthood's Twitter account to focus on every leftist cause under the sun even as *Roe* was collapsing. And it also explains why Planned Parenthood has struggled to adapt to the post-*Roe* world.

At first glance, Planned Parenthood seems to be doing okay. The abortion industry successfully leveraged the machine Richards built to raise money as well as to win elections and referenda in the wake of *Dobbs*. But a peek beneath the surface reveals an organization in crisis.

While media elites in Manhattan and San Francisco fawn over Planned Parenthood brass emphasizing intersectional politics, local Planned Parenthood staff have bigger fish to fry. Even as McGill Johnson pals around with Kamala Harris,[19] Jen Psaki,[20] and Al Sharpton,[21] local facility managers are trying to figure out how to deal with pro-life sidewalk counselors, undercover investigators, and an exodus of employees. The disconnect between Planned Parenthood headquarters and local Planned Parenthood facilities helps explain why more than 260 abortion workers have experienced conversion and left their jobs in response to 40 Days for Life vigils and more than 600 have walked away with the help of former Planned Parenthood employee of the year Abby Johnson.[22]

Planned Parenthood has also failed to win the hearts and minds necessary to build a lasting movement. The pro-abortion marches and rallies that sprang up immediately after the *Dobbs* leak and decision quickly tapered off. "In interviews with more than 50 advocates, analysts, abortion providers and legal experts, what emerged is a sense of the movement being forced to reckon with its mistakes," wrote Amy Little-field in *The New York Times*. "Chief among those mistakes was the relative neglect of grassroots groups."[23] *Teen Vogue* took its disenchantment with the abortion industry even far-ther, arguing that "the mainstream reproductive rights move-ment . . . no longer deserve[s] the bulk of our money, time, or attention."[24]

How could a juggernaut like Planned Parenthood become so ineffective at persuasion—especially with its hands on the political, media, and technological levers of power? "One of the critiques of the abortion-rights movement is that we put too much faith in the law, believing that it would protect the right to abortion," said American University "reproductive rights scholar" Tracy Weitz.[25]

This is to say, Planned Parenthood is bad at persua-sion because it never needed to persuade under *Roe*. With its five-decade judicial protection racket in the dumpster, Planned Parenthood is desperately trying to build a new post-*Roe* narrative based on manufactured talking points that just don't correspond with reality.

Don't be fooled by these five ridiculous myths abortion supporters have devised to save abortion in the post-*Roe* world:

Myth 1: Pro-Life Laws *Force* Women to Travel for Abortions

At her 20-week ultrasound, Heather Maberry learned her daughter Willow had anencephaly, a condition that results in death before or shortly after birth. "We came to the decision that we were going to try to get an abortion," she said.[26] But because Maberry lived in Kentucky—a state that protects unborn children from abortion with "very limited exceptions"—having an abortion close to home wasn't an option. Instead, she was referred to Chicago[27] for a 22- to 23-week abortion.

Maberry said she "came to the decision" to abort, but an ABC News article framed the matter differently: "Woman says she was forced to travel for an abortion despite her fetus's fatal condition."[28]

Abortion advocates love to use the word *force* for dramatic effect. "Force" sounds scary and mean and oppressive, so abortion supporters use the term every chance they get. Forced birth. Forced travel. Forced motherhood. However, Rush University Medical Center OB-GYN Dr. Sadia Haider acknowledged Maberry and her husband had other options. "The patients can choose what they want to do in this scenario," Haider said in the ABC News piece.[29]

A terminal prenatal diagnosis inflicts suffering you wouldn't wish on your worst enemy. The abortion industry exploits that pain to justify more than a million abortions every year without ever explaining why it's preferable to dismember a child than to allow the child to pass away naturally and without ever considering that abortion robs parents of the hope of holding their child, if only for a moment.

In Milwaukee, Wisconsin, Estrella's doctor diagnosed her son with a terminal genetic anomaly called trisomy 18 and referred her to a local abortion facility. Fortunately, 40 Days for Life leader Dan Miller was on the sidewalk when she arrived. Dan directed Estrella to a local pregnancy help center where she received real options, real health care, real *choice*.

"In the process of my pregnancy, I suffered a lot," Estrella recalled years later. "Always being told your son has trisomy 18, and he's not going to live, and there's no chance, obviously it hurts." But it also made her want to fight for her little boy. "Because who doesn't want the best for their children?" she asked.

Baby Martin Jr. survived only six hours after birth, but Estrella considered every second a gift. "It's not easy to be told your son is going to die. Thanks to that strong support, I got to meet my son. I am forever grateful."

The abortion industry robbed Maberry of that gift.

There's another reason the abortion industry loves the word *force*: It suggests that abortion is *inevitable*. "People everywhere want, need, and find ways to get abortions," wrote the pro-abortion Guttmacher Institute's Zara Ahmed. "Abortion bans are ineffective, harmful, and dangerous."[30]

Abortion advocates want pro-lifers to believe legal protections for unborn children are pointless because women will just travel for abortions. If they're going to abort anyway, why make it any harder? "Pregnant people are being forced to travel across state lines to get an abortion . . ." reads a Guttmacher Institute policy analysis.[31] "[A]s more and more states put bans in place . . . residents are going to have to travel out of state for care," said report coauthor Isaac Maddow-Zimet.[32]

But the abortion industry's predictions aren't borne out by the data, as many thousands of women in pro-life states have realized they don't have to abort their babies. In Texas alone, the number of babies born in 2022 increased by more than 16,000 compared with 2021.[33] This shouldn't be surprising. Research published in the *Journal of the American Medical Association* shows that when the nearest abortion facility is more than 25 miles away, abortions decrease by 25 percent.

When the distance increases to 100 miles, the number of abortions is cut in half.[34]

It's almost as though women aren't exactly clamoring to exercise their right to choose.

And this means abortion supporters will have to manufacture demand. With many states opting to protect human life in post-*Roe* America, businesses including JPMorgan Chase, Warner Brothers, Disney, Meta, Bank of America, Intuit, Starbucks, Nike, Walmart, and many others shared plans to cover employees' abortion-related travel expenses, while Google and Salesforce headline a list of companies that offer to *relocate* employees out of pro-life states.[35] Abortion supporters who argue that pro-lifers want to control women might want to take a look at the woke CEOs eager to pay women to get an abortion *so they can get back to work and carry their weight.* Are those CEOs willing to pay the travel costs of women who need to go out of state for, say, cancer treatment?

"It makes good business sense," said Civitech COO Sarah Jackel. "There's no reason we should be putting our employees in the position of having to choose between keeping their job or carrying out an unwanted pregnancy."[36]

In other words, "Congratulations on your pregnancy . . . and nice job you've got there. It would be a shame if something happened to it."

Myth 2: Overturning *Roe* Was a Steppingstone toward Banning Interracial Marriage

It's okay, you can laugh; it's funny. And yes, we wish we were making it up.

Nobody blames you for assuming race relations in America have already hit rock-bottom. But progressives used the overturning of *Roe* to find a new low. According to their rhetoric, the *Dobbs* ruling was the proverbial canary in the coal mine signaling that a variety of rights—including interracial marriage—were on the chopping block.

What does abortion have to do with interracial marriage? You have to squint to find the answer.

Justice Clarence Thomas's concurring opinion in *Dobbs* favored scrapping the Court's "substantive due process" approach to rights "that are not mentioned anywhere in the Constitution."[37] Abortion-friendly media and activists quickly proposed that he meant other rights not guaranteed explicitly by the Constitution should be rolled back:

- The ACLU released a podcast titled "How Dismantling *Roe* Puts Interracial Marriage at Risk."[38]
- Norreen Farrell, a "gender justice expert," said after *Dobbs,* "a number of privacy decisions [including interracial marriage] are potentially at risk if other justices in the court do not rein in this decision."[39] (If you can't trust a gender justice expert for honest, objective analysis, who *can* you trust?)
- University of California, Irvine, constitutional law professor Michele Goodwin said she fears white nationalism could lead racists to become county clerks who will presumably deny marriage licenses to interracial couples.[40]
- President Joe Biden signed into law a bill that protected interracial marriage.[41]

Of course, there is no threat to interracial marriage from Justice Thomas, *who is in an interracial marriage.* Nor from the public, as 94 percent of Americans approve of interracial marriage[42] (in a country where only 80 percent of Americans agree the earth is round).[43]

Abortion supporters know this. But when they bring up interracial marriage, they take the focus off the barbarity of abortion—and try to force you into a defensive position of denying that you're a racist. Don't take the bait by engaging in esoteric debates over the nuances of substantive due process. Instead, remind them that just about *nobody* opposes interracial marriage.

Myth 3: Protecting Unborn Babies from Abortion Is a Form of Slavery

Shortly after the demise of *Roe*, abortion advocates posited that if the Supreme Court couldn't find a right to abortion in the Fourteenth Amendment's due process clause, maybe it could find that right elsewhere in the Constitution. Pro-choicers then suggested abortion is protected by the Thirteenth Amendment to the U.S. Constitution, which ended slavery nationwide.

How in the world does the abolition of slavery equate to a right to kill unborn children? It's a stretch to say the least. The Thirteenth Amendment states, "Neither slavery nor involuntary servitude . . . shall exist within the United States, or any place subject to their jurisdiction."[44] Abortion supporters argue that pro-life laws unjustly compel expectant mothers into involuntarily serving their unborn children.

In other words, abortion advocates enjoy accusing pro-lifers of being "pro-forced birth" so much that they've made a legal argument out of it. "Mandated, forced or compulsory pregnancy contravenes . . . the Thirteenth Amendment's prohibition against involuntary servitude and protection of bodily autonomy," wrote professor of law Michele Goodwin.[45]

The assertion that bearing a child is akin to the experience of chattel slavery seems to be one of those pro-choice arguments that's so silly it doesn't deserve to be dignified with a response. But the argument has found favor in at least one corner of the federal judiciary. "[T]he Court might have held in *Dobbs* that some other provision of the Constitution [besides the Fourteenth Amendment] provided a right to access reproductive services," wrote U.S. District Court Judge Colleen Kollar-Kotelly in a brief order. "Of those provisions that might contain *some* right to access to such services, the Thirteenth Amendment has received substantial attention among scholars and, briefly, in one federal Court of Appeals decision."[46]

Would Judge Kollar-Kotelly consider child abuse and neglect laws that require parents to feed, clothe, and educate their children—*even involuntarily*—to enslave parents unconstitutionally?

Of course not. That is absurd. It's assumed that moms and dads refrain from committing violence against their children.

Now if pro-life legislation forced women to conceive children, Judge Kollar-Kotelly might have a point. But there's a big difference between *compelling* you to labor and *preventing* you from harming another person—particularly when the other person is your own child.

It's outrageous to compare forced hard labor in the fields to the most intimate relationship in the human experience: the bond between a mother and her baby. Anyone who suggests otherwise doesn't deserve to be taken seriously.

Myth 4: God Supports Abortion

This one is news to us (and to God!). The "God loves abortion" card is only played when substantive arguments for abortion are running low. While the pro-abortion movement isn't actually interested in what God thinks, selling abortion *only* to atheists isn't a viable economic strategy. So the abortion industry is working overtime to persuade Christians that God is okay with killing babies.

"It might come as a surprise that neither the Old Testament nor the New mentions abortion—not one word," wrote author Katha Pollitt.[47] Perhaps she missed "Thou shalt not kill" in the Ten Commandments. Or maybe she never read Psalm 22: "from my mother's womb you have been my God" (v. 10b NIV). More likely, Pollitt—who once announced, "I would vote for Joe Biden if he boiled babies and ate them"[48]—is just projecting her own hatred of children upon Almighty God.

Rev. Tim Ahrens, senior minister of First Congregational Church of Christ in Columbus, Ohio, went even farther, arguing that the Bible isn't just silent on abortion; it *supports* legal abortion. Ahrens filmed a television ad urging Ohioans to enshrine the right to abortion in the state constitution and claimed that legal protection for unborn children "runs counter to the Hebrew Scriptures and the Gospel of Jesus Christ."[49] Ahrens cited 1 Corinthians, which describes our bodies as "temples of the Holy Spirit," to infer "God blesses us to *have the right to choose over our body, and the freedom to make the decisions that are rightly [sic] protect our bodies for service in God's name.*"[50]

Unfortunately, in our opinion, Ahrens isn't the only unfaithful shepherd. Planned Parenthood even trots out a clergy advisory board to promote abortion to people of faith.[51] But the beliefs of these clergy members don't resemble anything like Christianity:

• Rev. Latishia James-Portis is a self-described "pleasure activist" who goes by the moniker "Rev. Pleasure."[52]

- Rev. Katey Zeh said she discovered her "call to ministry" as an abortion doula holding the hands of women getting abortions at Planned Parenthood.[53]
- Rev. Rebecca Todd Peters advocates reducing the world's population—especially the population of poor people.[54]
- Rev. Elle Dowd wrote a book describing her "hung[er] for revolution."[55]

Are these alleged clergy members simply leftist activists masquerading as ministers to dupe Christians into accepting their progressive agenda? We think so.

This phenomenon isn't limited to Planned Parenthood. It's now influential in Washington, DC. Rev. Raphael Warnock won election to the U.S. Senate while campaigning to keep abortion legal.[56] And in the White House, self-described devout Catholic[57] President Joe Biden—who once threatened to "shove my rosary beads down [the] throat" of any Republican who questioned his religious devotion[58]—campaigned for reelection by rallying for abortion.[59]

We don't want the president's Rosary between our tonsils, so we won't question whether he's religious or not, but obviously he's been an embarrassing scandal for the Catholic Church due to his long public support of abortion all while touting his Catholic faith. (Have you *ever* heard *anyone* describe himself as "devout" other than as an excuse for justifying killing babies?) Biden's comments suggest his devotion is aimed more toward abortion than toward Christianity.

Like pagans throughout history, modern-day abortion advocates have made killing children a sacrament. And this isn't hyperbole. The Satanic Temple promotes a "satanic abortion ritual," which concludes with a prayerlike "personal affirmation": "By my body, my blood / By my will, it is done."[60]

Within a year of the *Dobbs* decision, the Satanic Temple announced the opening of "The Samuel Alito's Mom's Satanic Abortion Clinic."[61] As of the writing of this book, plans are under way for a second abortion facility. Donors who contribute at least $666 can propose the facility's name.[62]

Nor is the Satanic Temple alone in its religious devotion to abortion. After the overturning of *Roe*, California artist and writer Jackie DesForges established the "Church of Potential Life," which incorporates Catholic imagery, an altar, and a mock Mass to literally worship abortion.[63]

It's hard to imagine this needs to be said, but pro-choice Christians ought to think twice about aligning themselves with *the devil.*

Myth 5: Nobody Survives Abortion

The case for abortion is typically rooted in the argument that a woman has a right to autonomy over her body. So it seems pro-lifers and pro-choicers could agree that when a baby survives abortion and is born alive, there's no reason to kill or abandon the child.

But across the country, pro-abortion governors have vetoed legislation that would require care for and would prevent infanticide against babies who survive their abortion appointments. "This bill is misleading and unnecessary," wrote Kansas governor Laura Kelly upon vetoing her state's born-alive infants protection act in 2023.[64]

Abortion advocates claim laws protecting abortion survivors try to solve a problem that doesn't exist. But they don't provide any evidence. In Kansas, the Department of Health and Environment does not maintain statistics on children born alive after failed abortions.[65]

This hasn't stopped the media from citing unnamed sources to claim that babies rarely survive their abortion appointments. "There is no recent national or Kansas data on live births during abortions, but medical experts say it's a very rare occurrence," wrote Rose Conlon of National Public Radio member station KMUW.[66] The *Kansas Reflector* described the born-alive bill as based on "the false pretense that 'failed abortions' are performed on infants that are capable of surviving."[67]

The *Arizona Mirror*'s coverage of similar legislation in the Grand Canyon State was even more outrageous: "Critics say the bill could mandate the torture of premature babies who have no chance of survival."[68] This isn't an opinion piece but a news article.

With journalists providing cover for infanticide, pro-abortion politicians across the country have thrown abortion survivors to the wolves with impunity. Fortunately, pro-lifers don't need to rely on anonymous experts and government bureaucrats to prove babies do survive abortions. We can talk to the abortion survivors themselves.

Melissa Ohden survived an attempted, forced late-term abortion—and lived to tell about it. "[W]hen I was delivered alive in that abortion procedure, there were actually demands made to leave me to die," she said. Melissa learned details about her entrance into the world from a nurse who was on duty that day and reported a fellow nurse rushed Melissa into the NICU, saying, "She just kept gasping for breath, and so I couldn't just leave her there to die."[69]

Contrary to Planned Parenthood's insistence that the existence of abortion survivors is "misinformation,"[70] Melissa has met hundreds of individuals who were aborted—and miraculously lived to tell about it.[71] "I think people would be absolutely stunned at the number," she said.[72]

Pinning down an exact number is difficult because comprehensive data does not exist. But the Centers for Disease Control released a report acknowledging at least 143 babies who died after surviving abortions between 2003 and 2014.[73] The state of Arizona reported 10 babies were born following failed abortions in 2017, and Florida reported 11.[74]

Research north of the border indicates U.S. numbers are likely seriously undercounted. According to research released by the Canadian Institute of Health Information, at least 1,155 babies were born alive following failed abortions between 2014 and 2021.[75] With the U.S. population more than eight times that of Canada,[76] it's not unreasonable to suspect the CDC's numbers are low by a couple of orders of magnitude. Applying Canadian abortion survival rates to U.S. abortion numbers, the Abortion Survivors Network estimates that more than 1,700 children are born alive each year in the United States following abortion attempts.[77]

Abortion supporters must lie about the reality that babies do survive abortion because the existence of abortion survivors reminds people of *what* the fetus being aborted actually is. And meeting those abortion survivors—like Melissa—reminds the world *who* the fetus is. Survivors also remind the world that every baby aborted would have had a face and a name and a personality—if only he or she had been given a chance.

The abortion industry can't risk this, so it denies that anybody survives abortion. "Our culture has wanted to avoid lives like mine," Melissa explained. "We're a bit of an inconvenient truth."[78]

❧

Don't let the abortion industry off the hook for being unprepared for the overturning of *Roe v. Wade*. Clumsy, hastily developed myths are no match for the truth.

What to Say to Debunk the Abortion Industry's Post-*Roe* Myths:

- Pro-life protections do save lives because women don't actually *need* to have abortions.
- Overturning *Roe* has nothing to do with interracial marriage, which *nobody* wants to ban.
- There's no Thirteenth Amendment right to abortion; laws that require parents to take care of their children— born or unborn—are not imposing slavery.
- Pro-abortion pastors are little more than progressive activists whose teachings bear no relation to Christianity.
- Babies do survive abortion—and they remind us that the world is a poorer place because more than a billion other souls didn't survive.[79]

CHAPTER 4

The Hardest of the Hard Cases

A dead thing goes with the stream,
but only a living thing can go against it.
— G. K. Chesterton[1]

Just days after the Supreme Court overturned *Roe v. Wade*, abortion advocates received great news. Well, actually, it was terrible news for everyone involved—except those looking to capitalize on a tragedy.

Headlines around the world reported that a nine-year-old Ohio girl had been raped and had become pregnant.[2] At the time, Ohio had enacted a fetal heartbeat law protecting the lives of unborn children once a heartbeat can be detected. The law took effect upon the reversal of *Roe*, so shortly after celebrating her tenth birthday, the girl traveled to Indiana for an abortion.[3]

Judging by mainstream media coverage, the tragedy wasn't the rape of a child who should be with her friends at the playground. The greater injustice was she had to travel 175 miles for the abortion. Abortion supporters quickly painted pro-lifers as cruel for their support of legal protections for unborn children. "She was forced to have to travel out of the state to Indiana to seek to terminate the pregnancy and maybe save her life," said President Joe Biden of the girl. "Ten years old—10 years old! Raped, six weeks pregnant, already traumatized, was forced to travel to another state."[4]

The *Guardian's* Moira Donegan went further, suggesting that protecting unborn children under the law and raping children are two sides of the same coin. Donegan proposed a statue be built in honor of the abortionist, whose "work brought her into the darkest realities of what men do to women—raping and impregnating them as children, making laws that will keep them pregnant against their will."[5]

It's not fun being compared to a child rapist just because you support equal protection under the law for children both before and after birth. But we don't need to fear the extreme, tragic cases that abortion advocates exploit to justify killing children.

If abortion supporters want to talk about child rape, let's talk.

But abortion advocates don't *actually* want to discuss those hard issues. They bring up child rape, incest, and other heinous crimes not to begin the conversation but to end it. Like an overmatched boxer who lacks the stamina and endurance for a full fight, they desperately throw rhetorical haymakers to try to land a knockout blow that ends the match in the first round.

When you muster up the courage to withstand the initial barrage, you can reveal that abortion supporters don't really care about nine-year-old rape victims if you ask some hard questions of your own:

- How does abortion heal a rape?
- Why is driving to a neighboring state a greater trauma than a violent procedure accompanied by an 81 percent increased risk of mental health problems?[6]

- Nobody would know about this child rape victim if she didn't have an abortion. Why is that?
- How did the rapist illegally enter the country,[7] and is anything being done to keep other child predators out?
- Why should we trust that the abortionist was acting in the child's best interests given that she spoke at a pro-abortion rally just days before performing the 10-year-old girl's abortion[8] and she was fined and reprimanded for violating the girl's privacy?[9]

The specific questions you ask will vary depending on the hard-case situation with which you're presented. But the principle remains the same: Why are you more concerned about defending abortion than about a barbaric crime committed against an innocent victim?

Remember these three points to remind abortion supporters that abortion does nothing to help abuse victims— even (and especially) in the most horrific cases.

Point 1: Abortion Perpetuates Abuse

Kristi Hofferber's biological mother was sexually abused by her own father for more than 20 years. That abuse resulted in Kristi's conception. Due to incest, Kristi's father was also her grandfather. Additionally, it led to the conceptions of Kristi's older sibling (who was miscarried because of the father's physical abuse) and four younger siblings, who were aborted.

As a product of incest, Kristi represents the type of "hard case" abortion advocates exploit to justify the shedding of innocent blood. But her biological mother's experience exposes the myth that abortion benefits abuse victims. Quite the opposite. Abortion enabled Kristi's father to destroy the evidence of his crimes and abuse her mother for decades without fear of being caught. "It's misplaced compassion [to support abortion in cases of rape and incest]," Kristi said. "With my birth mother, the abuse continued for over 20 years."

How, exactly, did abortion benefit Kristi's mother? And how many other victims of incest, abuse, and sex trafficking were denied a way out by legal abortion?

Even many self-identified pro-lifers support abortion to terminate pregnancies resulting from sexual abuse. "Sixty percent of those who are pro-life hold an exception," Kristi said. "So more than half of those standing *with* me make an exception for *my* life and those like me. But why shouldn't I have my own life just because of the way I was conceived?"

Certainly, some believe it a lesser evil—or at least more politically palatable—to sacrifice the life of a nameless, faceless child than to ask an abuse victim to carry the baby of her abuser. But Kristi provides a name, a face, *and* a voice to the "rape and incest" exception.

Kristi was placed for adoption. At 13 years old, she learned the truth about her conception in a newspaper article about her biological mother's legal case against her father. The article shocked Kristi, but it also led her to contemplate whether she should seek out a relationship with her biological mom. "The main concern I had with moving forward in my search was bringing up more trauma in her life," she said.[10]

But rather than retraumatizing Kristi's mother, the reunion was a joyful one. "[S]he welcomed me into her life, and in turn, it brought her some sense of closure," Kristi explained. "She had been told that it was likely that I did not survive due to an illness I had at birth."[11]

Abortion advocates will not admit that choosing life can be the means by which a woman triumphs over abuse. "People come back to me and say, 'I've really thought about this. I see where you're coming from, and you've actually changed my mind on the exceptions,'" Kristi recalled.

There's nothing compassionate about telling an abuse victim, "I'm sorry, but the best we can do for you—the best we're willing to do for you—is to take your money and kill your baby."

Kristi's life testifies that the circumstances of her conception don't diminish her human dignity.

Point 2: The Right to Abortion Becomes an Obligation to Abort

Elizabeth and Nicholas Brown were delighted to find out they were expecting, but because their first son had tuberous sclerosis, a genetic disease that caused him to have seizures, a geneticist brought up abortion, noting "a lot of . . . couples [facing challenging genetic conditions] consider terminating the pregnancy."[12]

While the couple's unborn child would have a 50-50 chance of having tuberous sclerosis, Elizabeth made it clear there was a 0 percent chance she'd end the life of her child. But even though she instructed her doctor never to bring up the subject of abortion again, she was asked about whether she had "thought about any options" again just three weeks later. "Are you talking about me killing my baby?" she asked the doctor. "Yes, terminating the pregnancy," the doctor responded. "You mean killing my baby," Elizabeth shot back.[13] Ultimately, the Browns' baby did not have tuberous sclerosis.

When abortion advocates argue that pro-lifers are extreme for opposing abortion even in cases of rape, incest, a maternal health condition, or because the child is sick or disabled, they set abortion as the default option for addressing difficult pregnancies. Abortion is expected. It's assumed. The woman's "choice" quickly gives way to social pressure.

And not only for the hardest cases. Abortion becomes the go-to option for much more run-of-the-mill, often temporary scenarios like financial troubles, job or education schedules, and relationship problems. Abortion advocates wash their hands of any sense of obligation to assist women who choose life because "they made their decision." Deadbeat boyfriends abandon the girlfriends they impregnated. Parents kick their daughters out of their homes.

The Browns were willing to fight for their little boy. *How many couples have lost a child to a choice that wasn't really theirs?*

Growing up, Paula Ilari didn't know—or care—much about abortion. She knew she wouldn't want to have an abortion. But that's about as far as she considered the issue.

Slowly and subtly, however, a community youth group she was involved with pressured her to get involved with America's leading abortion provider. "I started volunteering with Planned Parenthood in Memphis at 16," Paula remembered. "It started with the idea of, 'You care about women, right?' Who's going to say 'no'?"

Paula began helping organize Planned Parenthood outreach booths at events. She rose quickly through the ranks and within two years was counseling clients, administering HIV tests, and lobbying public officials. When she got to college, Paula still didn't know much about abortion, but she headed up the University of Memphis pro-abortion student group. The role brought her into dialogue with her school's Students for Life chapter, sowing the first seeds of conversion.

"I didn't have a change of heart right away," Paula recalled. "My heart had been hardened because I had been told for so long that pro-life people lie. But those conversations with the Tigers for Life stuck with me."

The seeds planted by her Students for Life adversaries sprouted in 2016 when Paula found herself in an unplanned pregnancy. "My life was not the ideal situation to bring a baby into the world, but I was really excited."

Paula's delight in becoming a mother came to an abrupt end when she miscarried—an experience that led her to question abortion for the first time. "I was just devastated," Paula said. "I remember having this tiny funeral with my family. I thought, *Babies are dying from abortion every day. They're not having funerals. Why does my child deserve to live, but someone else's doesn't?*"

The loss of her child made Paula's heart fertile soil for conversion. She drew close to the Lord and changed her lifestyle. Seven months later, she began dating again. "I had been grieving for a long time and I was feeling better," she said. "I wasn't seriously dating, just kind of getting out there again."

A guy Paula was getting to know invited her over to watch television. She accepted, but when he put his hands on her, she asked him to stop and headed for the door. In an instant, the situation spiraled out of control. The man's roommate intercepted Paula, pulled a gun on her, and told her she wasn't going anywhere. The two men held a gun to Paula's head and raped her.

Paula didn't smile again for weeks. Not until the pregnancy test she took came back positive. "I was overjoyed," Paula said. "I finally had a reason to live. My pain had suddenly developed a purpose."

Still, Paula wasn't done suffering yet. When her friends at church learned she was pregnant, they peppered her with questions: "When are you going to take care of this? When are you going to fix it? We can take care of this really quickly."

When Paula explained she was keeping her baby, congregants assumed she simply couldn't afford an abortion and offered to finance it themselves. One pressured Paula deep into her pregnancy—even offering to foot the $10,000+ bill for cross-country airfare and an abortion at one of America's few third-trimester abortion facilities. Fellow worshippers called Paula's child "the spawn of Satan" and accused Paula of "tainting the gene pool" by refusing an abortion. The verbal abuse was particularly cruel given that Paula herself was conceived in rape.

"They call themselves 'pro-choice,'" Paula said. "But they refused to accept my choice."

Even after Paula gave birth to her son, Caleb, the harassment continued. Congregants complained about Caleb's presence at church, claiming the newborn baby was a "bad influence" on other children. When her tormentors made a public Mother's Day donation to the abortion industry—a contribution Paula said was intended to make a statement about her decision to keep Caleb—Paula found a new faith community. Still, nearly two years after Paula left the church, the woman who offered to send her to New Mexico for a late-term abortion emailed again, insisting that Caleb should have been aborted.

The hateful response Paula received at her own church cemented her conversion. "While my heart had been starting to soften, it was my pregnancy that made me fully pro-life," she said. "I could no longer say people were pro-choice because they care about women after the horror they put me through."

Point 3: Abortion Doesn't Actually Help Women Even In—and Especially In—the Most Difficult Cases

Abortion advocates love to share long lists of crises in which women *need* abortion: rape, incest, life of the mother, poverty, domestic abuse, climate change (we're not kidding[14]), and many others. But all of these difficult cases assume that abortion will do something to solve the crisis at hand.

Question that assumption.

How does abortion heal a sexual assault? Will a woman's uterine cancer go into remission after an abortion? How will abortion help a woman escape poverty or abuse? What will abortion do to offset changing weather patterns?

Abortion advocates score a lot of political points by telling devastating stories—such as the nine-year-old rape victim—to justify killing babies. But we have stories of our own. And unlike the abortion industry's narratives, pro-life stories have happy endings.

Kayla was a high school sophomore sitting in the parking lot of a North Carolina abortion facility when the phone rang. It was her case worker calling to let her know that if she waited just a little bit longer before going through with the abortion, investigators would be able to collect the DNA evidence they'd need to confirm the identity of the rapist—a family member—responsible for her pregnancy.

"I was just sitting in silence in the back seat while they decided what to do with me," Kayla said.

She and her family decided abortion was the right decision for her even if she didn't really know what abortion was. "I thought it wasn't a baby until—I don't even know—maybe 15 weeks? And I wasn't that far along, so . . ." she trailed off.

Kayla was looking forward to getting it over with as soon as possible, which meant the case worker's suggestion to delay the abortion created a nervous tension in the car—a tension Grandma broke by suggesting, "Why don't we go to church?"

The family then made a pact: if the preacher talked about abortion or babies or anything of the kind, they'd take it as a sign and back out of the now-rescheduled abortion appointment. Nearly an hour into the service, Kayla thought she was in the clear. "The sermon wasn't over, but in my head, it's almost over," she remembered. "He hasn't said anything about abortion. This time tomorrow I'll be done. This will be behind me. I'll be fine."

But Pastor Tony wasn't done speaking, and neither was God.

The preacher suddenly recounted how he had been driving down the street where the city's Planned Parenthood is located and saw someone on the sidewalk holding a 40 Days for Life "Pray to End Abortion" sign in the middle of a torrential downpour. "He basically yelled that abortion is wrong— *no matter the circumstance*," Kayla said. "It caught us all off guard. We were distraught because we all wanted for me to go get an abortion and just be done with it."

Kayla and her family had intended to leave church quickly and quietly. But having been hit by a spiritual two-by-four, they lingered until one of the church pastors approached them to ask what was wrong and how he could help. Kayla and her family shared everything.

"Have you considered adoption?" the pastor asked.

"Lord, please let there be something in my voice that tells this young girl that we're the family for this baby, that I'm supposed to be this child's mom," Felisha Mims prayed before dialing Kayla's number to set up a visit at which Kayla would vet Felisha and her husband, Wayne, as possible adoptive parents.

The phone call led to a face-to-face visit in which Felisha gave Kayla a book she had prepared to introduce herself and her husband to any birth moms considering placing a baby for adoption. The back of the book listed several promises the Mimses would make to the prospective birth mom and baby—vows to love the child, to teach the child about God, and to care for and protect the child no matter what. Felisha noticed Kayla rubbing her hand over the cover of the book that bore those promises.

Before parting ways, Kayla moved her hand from the book to her womb and announced, "Hey, little one in there. This is your new mom." She then turned to address Felisha. "I don't know what it is, but there was something in your voice when we talked on the phone the other night that told me that you're supposed to be the mama for this baby."

"I held myself together the best I could," Felisha remembered.

Felisha and Wayne supported Kayla throughout her pregnancy, driving her to her prenatal visits, ultrasounds, and birthing classes. They soon became inseparable. "Felisha and Wayne basically took care of me," Kayla said. "I spent weekends with them. I went to church with them. They treated me like family, not just someone who would be there temporarily. I felt more at home and safe with them than I ever had." They also watched movies and baked cookies together, and Kayla had her own room at the Mimses' house.

One night, they finished watching a sad movie that made everyone cry, so Wayne suggested an ice cream run. The seemingly ordinary moment prompted an extraordinary realization. "At that moment I realized that I just loved them as people and as my *family*," Kayla said. "That's who they were to me. They were my family."

Felisha was in the delivery room for the birth of Abigail Hope, an experience that reaffirmed Kayla's adoption decision. "Watching them hold her and love her—and the way they looked at her—I just knew that this was the best choice I could have made for Abigail. Wayne and Felisha made me feel safe, and they loved me like I had never been loved before."

Ultimately, Kayla asked Felisha and Wayne to adopt her. They tearfully accepted the request, meaning Abigail is Kayla's daughter by blood and sister through adoption. The adoption provides a storybook ending, but is the day-to-day experience of being the sister to your biological daughter awkward? "Absolutely not," Kayla said. "Abigail could not be more my sister. She irritates me like a little sister. I love her, and I protect her. I would die for her."

That last sentence packs a little extra punch given that Abigail was a phone call away from dying for Kayla just a few short years ago.

"Looking back, abortion would've stripped me completely of anything I had left," Kayla said. "It would've taken away more than it would've given me. Because seeing Abigail run around, hearing her laugh, her running up and hugging me—oh my goodness! I would've missed out."

What to Say When Abortion Advocates Bring Up Hard Cases:

- Abortion perpetuates abuse.
- The choice of abortion becomes an obligation to abort.
- Abortion doesn't help or heal women in difficult circumstances.

CHAPTER 5

You Don't Care about Born Children

An ad hominem attack against an intellectual, not against an idea, is highly flattering. It indicates that the person does not have anything intelligent to say about your message.

— Nassim Nicholas Taleb, Essayist and Scholar[1]

This is a fun one.

It's news to pro-lifers that, for some reason, we only care about children until birth. Yes, we love these precious unborn babies whom we can neither see nor talk to. We stand up for them, sacrifice for them, cast our votes on Election Day for them. And then the moment they're born, we look into their eyes, scowl, slam the door in their cute little faces, and wish them a life of misery and suffering.

It sounds strange and even made up . . .

. . . because it is. Don't let this lazy ad hominem attack trap you.

I (Shawn) was on a plane, and as often happens when I travel, abortion came up with the passenger next to me. A man in his early 30s said the classic line, "The problem with pro-life people is that they only care about children until they're born."

I didn't launch into how great pro-life people are. I didn't tell him how many babies pro-lifers adopt or how we love sick children or serve food at the soup kitchen. Instead, I burst into laughter.

We are all tempted to justify ourselves and our fellow pro-lifers, and too many pro-life people (us included!) start defending how much we love humanity. ***Stop this! For real! We must stop this. Do not defend how amazing pro-life people are (and they are!) and lower ourselves to treat this absurd accusation with a response.***

Instead, give it the attention it initially deserves: laughter.

I couldn't stop laughing in response to the guy on the plane. He kept asking, "What?" And now he was smiling too.

I said, "You're right."

"About what?" he replied.

"Pro-life people don't care about kids once they're born," I answered. "You got me."

The man started to chuckle. I said, "I'm serious; I hate kids. I don't even like my own kids." At this point, the guy was cracking up, so I dug in.

"It goes far beyond my own kids. I mean, I love seeing ultrasound pictures, but there is nothing more enjoyable to me than seeing those starving kids suffering in Africa or hearing about another abandoned kid sent off to the orphanage. It's like Christmas to me; it really is! I usually celebrate suffering born children with a big piece of cake and a dry red wine. My wife is the same way!"

The guy was rolling in laughter at this point, "All right, all right, I get it. Dang, man, that's not the response I thought I'd get."

He was laughing because it's funny. Ignorant, stupid, and irrational arguments are funny when you play them out to their natural conclusions. The accusation you don't care about born children is a purely emotional, baseless attack designed to put pro-life people on the defensive. It's absurd and should be treated as such.

I followed up with a point that has never let me down.

"So you believe unborn children have fewer rights than born children, correct?" I asked.

"Yes."

"And you do not believe a mother should be allowed to kill her six-month-old or kindergartner because the child is crying or acting out?"

"No, that would be abhorrent."

"So because the unborn are not yet fully developed, they are less human than the born and don't enjoy the same rights as the born?" I continued.

"Yes, they get fewer rights."

"And that justifies abortion?"

"Yes."

"Okay, here's the deal, and it's true throughout the history of the world," I responded before explaining to him.

Point 1: People Who Want to Kill People *Can't* Claim They Care *More* Than the People Who *Don't* Want to Kill People

The Nazis don't give us ethics classes, and we don't learn about equality in the workplace from slave owners. The convicted child molester doesn't get to accuse the cops of not caring for children. Neither do abortion doctors, abortion workers, abortion supporters, or pro-abortion politicians get to tell us they care more about babies while simultaneously dehumanizing and killing them.

History makes it clear: those who affirm life and freedom care more about people than those who deny life and freedom. This is neither difficult nor complicated.

Sometimes abortion advocates will object, arguing that they do care about people—the unborn child, however, is not fully human and, therefore, not a person. We cover the humanity of the baby in the first *What to Say When*. Here, we will rephrase our point:

> **The people who dehumanize a group of people to justify killing can't argue that they care *more* about people.**

The case for life doesn't make sense if abortion doesn't kill a baby, but it does. So we pro-lifers have no obligation to prove we love humanity—especially to those who support destroying humanity at its most vulnerable, defenseless stage.

Point 2: Nobody Is More Alone and Vulnerable Than an Unborn Baby

The argument that abortion supporters want to help women and children and that pro-life people don't made a major comeback after *Roe* was overturned. Abortion supporters and media outlets parroted it over and over again.

A *HuffPost* headline read, "George Carlin Nailed Conservative Hypocrisy on Abortion 25 Years Ago."[2] The article cited a comedy routine in which Carlin says:

> They're all in favor of the unborn. They would do anything for the unborn, but once you're born, you're on your own [as he points his middle finger upward]. Pro-life conservatives are obsessed with the fetus from conception to nine months. After that, they don't wanna know about you. They don't wanna hear from you. No nothing!

No neonatal care, no day care, no Head Start,
no school lunch, no food stamps, no welfare, no
nothing. If you're pre-born, you're fine. If you're
in preschool, you're f——d.[3]

This is intended to be a "gotcha" moment, which is both
sensational and comical. The entertainment factor allows
Carlin's point to escape being examined or questioned. But
it's dishonest to argue that pro-lifers treat children as on their
own after birth. So let's examine this concept of "on your
own."

Consider the babies scheduled to be aborted—and who
will *not* help them:

- Their own mothers
- Their own fathers (even if a dad doesn't want the abor-
  tion, he has no legal right to stop it)
- Their government, which will pay for the abortion in
  most countries
- The only doctor who will ever examine them
- The only nurses they will ever encounter
- Most, if not all, of the extended family members who
  don't even know they exist
- Local, state, and national politicians who only accept
  that they exist in the abstract
- Their fellow citizens who don't know they exist and can
  neither see nor hear them

And, of course, they are unable to help themselves.
They are unable to mentally think their way out of it.
They cannot speak, and if they do, no one hears them.
They cannot take direction from someone speaking to
them.

Review this list of who and what is stacked against the unborn child scheduled to be aborted.

Who could be more on their own than abortion-bound babies?

Imagine children around the world in the most hopeless of circumstances (and we've encountered the worst of the worst in our work). The unborn child scheduled for abortion is *still* more alone. Every born child, no matter how desperate, has someone who would—or at least *could*—stand up for her. This entire list can only apply to an unborn child.

I'm not pointing this out to dismiss children who suffer after birth. I'm also not pointing it out to refute George Carlin, God rest his soul. I'm highlighting the fact that the *child slated for abortion is the loneliest of any human who has ever lived.*

George's rant is just a political wish list of all the programs he thinks government should provide. It's an important political, fiscal, and moral conversation to have, and many states are having it. Conservatives are much more willing now than in the past to support programs to help women, children, and the poor. American taxpayers do more to care for the vulnerable than ever before. And that's before we account for the approximately 3,000 pregnancy resource centers that offer free medical care and alternatives to abortion.[4] Pregnancy centers now outnumber abortion providers 5 to 1.

Some say government should do more and others less; it's an American debate that has gone on forever and will continue as long as America exists. What has changed about the debate is now one side says, "If the government doesn't provide particular services, we will kill the people who need them."

Even the biggest expansions of government services in history—like FDR's New Deal and LBJ's Great Society—didn't require this type of hostage-taking. Who would trust someone who makes such an ultimatum? They advocate for killing the unborn as they push to get more care and help for the born. It's like advocating for slavery as you lobby for more job opportunities for freed slaves. We don't trust that you actually care about black people, and we're not buying that you adore children.

You cannot disregard an unborn child set to be dismembered and sucked through a vacuum and then consider yourself to be a heroic child advocate for the same child once she passes through the birth canal, when something magically happens and you become the most compassionate, helpful, sacrificial child caregiver humanity has ever seen. It's unbelievable.

Where did such an insane notion come from?

Roe v. Wade.

The legalization of abortion transformed killing into a legitimate political solution. We've never done this as a country. Even with slavery, no one argued we should kill slaves instead of freeing them. A few advocated it, but they were fringe nuts to whom no one paid attention (thankfully).

The notion that the government should either provide services for its citizens or kill those citizens was brought to us by abortion. It cannot be given credibility, but it is an excellent opportunity to highlight the consistency of the pro-life position. Caring for children before *and* after they're born is the only logical approach.

Denying benefits leading to the killing of citizens is one of the many bizarre things we apply to abortion.

Point 3: There's No Need to Pit Vulnerable Groups Against Each Other; We Can Love Them All

There's nothing new about attributing bad motives to well-intentioned people. Here are a few examples:

- People who oppose war must hate the military.
- Death penalty opponents have more compassion for criminals than victims.
- Those who support building a border wall must hate immigrants.
- Immigration advocates don't care about national security.
- Climate change skeptics don't care about the environment.

It's absurd to suggest that if you care about one particular marginalized group, then you must hate all others. Have fun exposing the absurdity by sharing hypothetical examples that bring this mentality to its logical end:

- Mother Teresa didn't care about fed children.
- Environmentalists don't care about Jupiter's climate.
- PETA loves animals, so it must hate azalea plants.
- Politicians who provide poor citizens with social-ized medicine hate citizens who have private health insurance.
- Athletes who visit dying patients in St. Jude Children's Research Hospital don't care about kids who can't read.

But what if abortion supporters are right? What if we are indeed self-righteous bigots hiding behind unborn children?

What if we gather all pro-lifers at a conference in Washington, DC, and proclaim:

> We, the pro-life movement, declare that once you pass though the birth canal, we couldn't care less about you. We don't care about your poverty, hunger, neglect, drug problem, or abusive parents. You are on your own. We don't care. You were born alive. Be grateful and leave us alone!

Would this statement justify abortion?

Why do abortion supporters *need* pro-lifers to neglect born children to justify killing unborn children? If there's nothing wrong with abortion, then our feelings, beliefs, and opinions are irrelevant and a distraction from the question of the morality of abortion. Why focus on us? Who cares whether we love or hate born children? The morality of abortion doesn't depend on whether we are Hitler or St. Vincent de Paul. It depends on what the unborn child is. And if the unborn child is a living human being—as science proves—you don't need to be a beacon of virtue to proclaim that killing the living human being is wrong.

One of the most effective ways to respond to absurd arguments is to question those arguments:

- Can we kill people solely because we think others don't care enough about them?
- Can we justifiably kill people because other people don't care enough about people *we* care about?
- Would the Nazis have been justified in killing Jews because they felt the Jews didn't care enough about Muslims?

- Were plantation owners justified in owning slaves because the working conditions in northern factories were so bad?
- Were the Aztecs in the clear for human sacrifice because they believed the Spanish were greedy?
- Can we murder gun store owners because we believe they don't care about school shootings?

Of course not. We can never use our perception of someone else's apathy to justify evil—especially murder. Abortion is murder, and no mistreatment or neglect of another human being can excuse it.

❧

Unlike many facets of the abortion debate, the "you don't care about born children" argument can be handled with humor. Don't be too serious and don't give credibility to a ridiculous claim that doesn't deserve it.

That said, remain respectful. Many abortion supporters are moved by a false—but sincere—compassion. We aren't looking to accuse them of hating unborn children but to guide them to consistency. They really do care about born children; therefore, they really should care about unborn children.

The unborn child scheduled to be aborted has a long list of people, institutions, and their own weaknesses working against them. Again, they are the most alone humans ever to have lived.

But they are not *totally* alone.

They have you.

You can decide whether they are totally alone. You can help give them a chance at life. You can be their hands, feet, and voices. You can help overcome the many influences pushing for their deaths.

They are weak, silent, and helpless.

You are not.

What to Say When You're Accused of Caring Only about Unborn Children:

- People who want to kill people *can't* claim they care *more* than the people who *don't* want to kill people.
- Nobody is more alone and vulnerable than an unborn baby.
- There's no need to pit vulnerable groups against each other. We can love them all.

CHAPTER 6

Decodifying the "Codify *Roe*" Onslaught

*I learned things this week . . . pretty basic things that I did not
know about abortion. Like in Europe—the modern countries
of Europe—are way more restrictive than we are. . . . If you are
pro-choice, you would like it a lot less in Germany and Italy
and France and Spain and Switzerland.*

—Bill Maher, HBO Talk Show Host[1]

With one sentence at an otherwise unremarkable campaign
event back in the summer of 2007, then-Sen. Barack
Obama changed the abortion debate in the United States for
years to come. "The first thing I'd do as president is sign the
Freedom of Choice Act," Obama told a group of Planned Parenthood supporters.[2]

One of the most radical pieces of pro-abortion legislation ever introduced, the Freedom of Choice Act (FOCA)
declared, as federal policy, "every woman has the fundamental right to choose to bear a child, to terminate a pregnancy
prior to fetal viability, or to terminate a pregnancy after fetal
viability when necessary to protect the life or health of the
woman."[3] In other words, governments at the federal, state,

and local levels would be powerless to establish even the most basic protections for unborn children, and pro-life laws already on the books would be instantly erased.

"FOCA would abolish virtually every existing state and federal limitation on abortion, including parental consent and notification laws for minors, state and federal funding restrictions on abortion, and conscience protections for pro-life citizens working in the health care industry—protections against being forced to participate in the practice of abortion or else lose their jobs," wrote Princeton Professor Robert George.[4]

Professor George's assessment wasn't conservative fear-mongering. Abortion advocates salivated at the opportunity to "sweep away hundreds of anti-abortion laws [and] policies," as the National Organization for Women put it.[5]

FOCA was nothing new. The first version of the bill was introduced in 1989.[6] During the next two decades, Congress repeatedly reintroduced it—with increasingly radical modifications.[7] Nor was FOCA the first bill of its kind. The National Abortion Act, similarly designed to legalize abortion and override state abortion laws nationwide, had been introduced even before *Roe v. Wade*.[8]

What *was* new was a serious presidential contender throwing his support behind FOCA. Historically, FOCA and its predecessors all died on the vine without ever coming close to passage. Obama's support gave abortion advocates hope that the bill might finally become law.

This wasn't your grandmother's abortion debate anymore. Only 15 years earlier, Arkansas Gov. Bill Clinton won the presidency campaigning to make abortion "safe, legal, and rare."[9] The clever phrase assured abortion fence-sitters that Clinton wasn't going to make abortion a crime but he wasn't an abortion zealot either.

However, while Clinton *ran* as an abortion moderate, he *governed* as an abortion zealot. Clinton twice vetoed bipartisan bills to ban partial-birth abortion, a procedure that involves partially delivering a late-term baby before brutally killing the child.[10] As a measure of how out of the mainstream Clinton's vetoes were, even future President Joe Biden and future Senate Majority Leader Harry Reid voted to ban the barbaric procedure in 1995[11] and again in 1997![12]

By the time Clinton's wife, Hillary, ran for the Democratic presidential nomination in 2008, their party had grown increasingly intolerant of dissent when it came to supporting abortion. There was no longer room in the party for talk of making abortion "rare." So as extreme as the Clintons' record on abortion was, Obama's embrace of FOCA allowed him to outflank Hillary to the left on the issue.

It worked. Obama's abortion extremism was red meat for his party's base, helping him win an upset victory against the former first lady and the general election against Republican senator John McCain.

Pro-lifers were understandably anxious when Obama entered the White House in January 2009, and they responded with remarkable opposition to FOCA. A *Politico* article described the first three months of the Obama presidency as "like an extended recruiting drive for the anti-abortion movement."[13] Christians flooded the halls of Congress with postcards urging legislators to stop FOCA from passing. Bishop Paul Loverde from the Catholic Diocese of Arlington, Virginia, personally delivered nearly 200,000 postcards to his state's congressional delegation.[14] Pennsylvania senator Bob Casey Jr. alone received more than 100,000.[15]

The pro-life backlash succeeded, and Obama quickly backed down from his campaign-trail promise to enact FOCA. "Now, the Freedom of Choice Act is not my highest legislative priority," Obama said just months after taking office. "I believe that women should have the right to choose, but I think that the most important thing we can do to tamp down some of the anger surrounding this issue is to focus on those areas that we can agree on."[16]

"[T]he Freedom of Choice Act has all but disappeared," wrote a *PolitiFact* analysis. "We rate this a Promise Broken."[17]

Obama should have been able to pass FOCA. For most of his first two years in office, his party enjoyed a massive majority in the House of Representatives and a filibuster-proof supermajority in the Senate. But grassroots pro-lifers held the line, and they didn't allow Obama to have a second chance to enact FOCA. The Democrats lost the House in the landslide 2010 midterm elections and didn't win it back for the remainder of Obama's presidency. When Donald Trump won a surprise victory in the 2016 presidential election, it ensured that FOCA was dead for at least another four years.

Obama's failure to enact FOCA preserved state and local governments' ability to at least restrict abortion. But it's understandable that FOCA wasn't the hill Democrats wanted to die on. *Roe* was the law of the land. Five of the nine U.S. Supreme Court justices were pro-abortion—and George W. Bush appointee Chief Justice John Roberts later proved unwilling to scrap *Roe*. Meanwhile, the pro-abortion majority on the court soon got younger, as Obama appointed pro-abortion Justices Sonia Sotomayor and Elena Kagan to replace retiring Justices David Souter and 90-year-old John Paul Stevens.

Even without FOCA, *Roe* was safe, and abortion remained legal in all 50 states for the foreseeable future.

Ironically, it was Trump's shocking victory that November that set in motion efforts to resurrect FOCA. The story begins with the February 2016 death of pro-life Justice

Antonin Scalia, which put a pro-life majority on the Supreme Court even farther out of reach. Republican Senate Majority Leader Mitch McConnell blocked Obama nominee Merrick Garland from replacing Scalia. But pro-lifers weren't out of the woods yet. With Hillary Clinton apparently coasting into the White House in that fall's election, it was only a matter of time before Scalia would be replaced by a pro-abortion justice. The setback would delay a pro-life Supreme Court majority by a generation—*at least.*

Astonishingly, Clinton lost both the election and the opportunity to cement the pro-abortion Supreme Court.

Trump first kept Scalia's seat pro-life by replacing the late justice with pro-life Neil Gorsuch. Next, Trump tapped pro-life Brett Kavanaugh to replace retiring pro-abortion Justice Anthony Kennedy in 2018. But as Trump's term wound down, it appeared the 2020 election would arrive with the Supreme Court still one justice short of a pro-life majority.

Then just weeks before a tight election Trump ultimately lost, staunchly pro-abortion Justice Ruth Bader Ginsburg succumbed to cancer. Like Obama, Trump found himself with an election-year vacancy on the high court. Unlike Obama, Trump's party held control of the Senate, empowering him to confirm a justice of his choosing regardless of which way the election went.

Trump had saved Judge Amy Coney Barrett for just this moment. The abortion industry and its friends in the Senate couldn't credibly attack a brilliant mother—parenting seven children while excelling at a demanding career—as a member of the dreaded "patriarchy." Besides, after viciously attacking Kavanaugh's character during his confirmation hearings two years earlier, Democrats had already spent whatever political capital they might have used to derail the nomination. Judge Barrett became Justice Barrett one week before Election Day.[18]

Progressives who had long adored Obama suddenly turned on him for failing to pass FOCA when he had the chance. "Barack Obama Blasted for Not Codifying *Roe v. Wade*" read a *Newsweek* headline the day after *Roe* was overturned.[19] The Supreme Court's *Dobbs v. Jackson Women's Health Organization* decision allowed states across the country to protect the lives of unborn children legally. To restore abortion nationwide, abortion supporters would need to revive FOCA.

They learned some critical lessons from their failure to pass it back in 2009. First and foremost, they recognized they need to frame the legislation differently this time around. When Obama took office, pro-lifers quickly defined the terms of the debate. FOCA was a radical departure from the status quo because it

- eliminated the freedom states had long enjoyed to enact modest, common-sense abortion regulations within their borders;
- was a sweetheart deal to enrich the controversial abortion industry; and
- stripped pro-life medical professionals of their freedom not to participate in abortion—and might even lead to the closure of religiously affiliated hospitals.

In the post-*Roe* era, strategically minded abortion advocates have grown more restrained in their messaging. They're still pushing pro-abortion bills just as revolutionary as FOCA—if not more so. But they're downplaying the ambition of their own proposals. The abortion lobby has cleverly branded FOCA-like legislation as simply "codifying" *Roe*. It's a tactic designed to cloak abortion extremism as mere preservation of a status quo that had been in place since January 22, 1973.

Don't be deceived. Codifying *Roe* is just FOCA reheated in the microwave. Remember these points as you explain why legislation to "codify *Roe*" is dangerous.

Point 1: Codifying *Roe V. Wade* Would Impose One of the Most Barbaric Abortion Laws in the World upon All 50 States

Abortion supporters frequently cite public opinion polls that suggest most Americans support the Supreme Court's *Roe* decision—and oppose the *Dobbs* decision that overturned it. But it's worth noting that many Americans don't actually know what *Roe* said and did.

"The polling on *Roe v. Wade* is very misleading and very unhelpful in terms of gauging what Americans really think about abortion," said Dr. Michael New, assistant professor of social research at the Busch School of Business at the Catholic University of America. "Some people don't even know what *Roe v. Wade* is about. There was a poll that found something like 15 percent of Americans thought that *Roe v. Wade* had to do with school desegregation."

New said a second problem with pro-*Roe* public polling is even Americans who do know what *Roe* is about lack full comprehension of just how extreme the decision was. "People don't really understand the complete implications," he explained. "*Roe v. Wade* effectively legalized abortion on demand in all 50 states throughout all nine months of pregnancy. Some of the media coverage around *Roe* suggests it only made abortion legal in the first trimester."

When abortion supporters clamor for codifying *Roe*, don't assume they know what they're talking about. Educate them, then ask them some questions:

- Codifying *Roe* would allow for abortion—*just because the unborn child is a girl*. Do you really want to force that on all 50 states?
- Codifying *Roe* would allow aborting babies—*just because they are black*. Is that okay with you?
- Did you know even Justice Ruth Bader Ginsburg admitted that *Roe* "ventured too far"?[20]
- Codifying *Roe* would force all 50 states to allow elective abortion after 20 weeks' gestation, a policy shared by only six other countries on the planet—including China and North Korea.[21] How do you feel about that?
- Only one in three Americans want abortion to be legal after the first trimester.[22] Why should Congress pass a law that goes so much farther?

Nearly five decades living—and more than 60 million babies dying—under *Roe* was bad enough. But as we'll see, proposals to codify the ruling are much, much worse than even *Roe* was.

Point 2: Proposals to Codify *Roe* Are *Far* More Extreme Than *Roe* Was

In 2019, New York Gov. Andrew Cuomo ordered landmarks throughout his state to be lit up in celebration.[23]

Did the Yankees win another World Series? No, the now-disgraced former governor ordered landmarks illuminated in pink to celebrate his signing of the Reproductive Health Act.

The Empire State has one of America's highest abortion rates,[24] with more than 100,000 children aborted every year.[25] In New York City, more black babies are aborted than born.[26] The state is home to more than 100 abortion facilities.

For Governor Cuomo and the New York legislature, none of it was enough.

Justice Brett Kavanaugh had joined the Supreme Court just three months earlier, and abortion supporters could see that *Roe* was on thin ice. So Cuomo launched a preemptive strike, signing one of the country's most fanatical abortion bills into law. He claimed the Reproductive Health Act merely codified *Roe* at the state level.[27] But it went much farther, decriminalizing late-term abortions and allowing nonphysicians to perform abortions.[28] It even removed legal protections for babies who are born alive following botched abortions.[29]

With Trump in office, there was no chance to enact FOCA at the federal level, so Cuomo took matters into his own hands. New York wasn't the only state to use the push to codify *Roe* as a pretext for enacting militantly pro-abortion public policies:

- Rhode Island repealed its partial-birth abortion ban as well as state-level restrictions on abortion.[30]
- Massachusetts' "Roe Act" legalized abortion even into the third trimester of pregnancy in more cases and allowed 16- and 17-year-old girls to get abortions without parental consent.[31]
- Illinois also dropped its partial-birth abortion ban, deregulated abortion facilities, ended waiting periods for abortion, required private health insurance plans to fund abortion, dropped abortion reporting requirements, and even eliminated requirements to investigate the deaths of women killed by abortion.[32]

- Vermont passed legislation making it illegal to "inter-fere[e] with or restrict . . . the right of an individual to terminate the individual's pregnancy" at any point in the pregnancy.[33]
- Colorado[34] and Illinois[35] enacted laws declaring "a fertilized egg, embryo, or fetus does not have independent . . . rights."

That's just a sample of the uncivilized proposals introduced and passed at the state level. When *Roe* fell, the bloodlust only increased as states tripped over themselves to become "abortion sanctuary states," apparently ignorant of how history judges those who systematically dehumanize entire segments of their population.

- California allocated more than $200 million to train new abortion "clinicians" and to build and expand new abortion facilities while also budgeting $20 million for nonresidents to travel to the Golden State for abortions.[36]
- Nevada Republican Gov. Joe Lombardo won a major national pro-life endorsement—and then signed into law legislation to protect abortion providers.[37]
- Colorado banned abortion pill reversal.[38]
- Minnesota established that abortion is a "fundamental right."[39]

While efforts to enact FOCA-like policies ramped up at the state level during the Trump administration, they returned to the federal stage with the election of President Joe Biden. In 2021, the House of Representatives introduced and passed the Women's Health Protection Act (WHPA), again under the guise of codifying *Roe*.[40] The WHPA was the natural successor to FOCA. And some abortion proponents said the quiet part out loud, admitting that—like FOCA—the WHPA was designed to go much farther than *Roe*. "To those who say we want to go back in a time machine to the day before *Dobbs*, that was still a bad day," said Mini Timmaraju, president of National Abortion Rights Action League (NARAL).[41]

This legislation would:

- allow nonphysicians to perform abortions.[42]
- prohibit states from requiring ultrasounds and waiting periods before a woman can have an abortion.[43]
- invalidate many laws that significantly protect the health and safety of abortion clients.[44]
- threaten parental involvement laws for minors seeking abortions.[45]
- endanger existing state and federal laws that protect medical professionals' and hospitals' rights not to participate in abortion.[46]

The WHPA passed the House of Representatives.[47] In the Senate, it failed when Democrats fell two votes short of eliminating the filibuster. Once past the filibuster, the Democrats still would have needed one more vote to pass the bill.[48] Hearkening back to Obama's 2007 stump speech, Biden promised that the first bill he'd sign into law would be the WHPA—*if* Democrats could maintain control of the House and gain the two senators needed to break the filibuster and cast a 51st "yea" vote on the legislation.[49] They didn't accomplish either objective. But while the WHPA didn't pass, it came dangerously close to wiping out virtually every abortion restriction in the land.

Point 3: Progress Means Killing *Roe v. Wade*, Not Babies

The night before the Supreme Court heard oral arguments in *Dobbs*, I (Steve) flew to Jackson, Mississippi, to speak at a prayer rally in front of the lone abortion facility still open in the state. After the rally, a national television network reporter asked me just how pro-lifers planned to start supporting women facing unexpected pregnancies if *Roe* were overturned and abortion ended in the state.

"We won't need to *start* doing anything," I explained. "There is already a wide variety of resources available to help women get through their pregnancies and beyond and to *thrive*."

The reporter didn't seem to understand, asking, "But where will women facing unplanned pregnancies go for help?"

I elaborated on pregnancy help centers, maternity homes, job and financial assistance, health care options, parenting classes, material support, and many other free or low-cost resources, which have long been available—often through the generosity of pro-life Christians. It was a comprehensive answer, but still the reporter asked, "Sure, but could you just tell me what you'll do to help women if *Roe* gets overturned?"

By this point, I began to empathize with Peter after the resurrection when the Lord repeatedly asked him, "Simon, son of Jonah, do you love Me more than these?" (John 21:15 NKJV). And so, distressed that the reporter had asked me a third time, "How will you help women if *Roe* is overturned?" I responded, "Look, you can ask me the same question all night, and I'm going to give you the same answer: We're going to continue to support women in need before, during, and after they deliver their children."

The conversation ended, but the phenomenon continues: Abortion supporters expect pro-lifers to apologize for the overturning of *Roe*. They insist that *only* abortion can help an expectant mother in need. And they repeatedly insist that federal, state, and local governments "merely" codify *Roe*.

They're on the wrong side of history.

The United States of America has a long and painful history of bitterly divisive debates over which segments of our population are entitled to basic human rights. From slavery to mistreatment of indigenous Americans to Jim Crow to the internment of Japanese Americans, history has *never*—not once—looked kindly upon those who sought to dehumanize their fellow man or woman. It's easy for self-styled progressives to cast judgment upon sins of the past. They should tremble as they consider that future generations will look back upon abortion supporters with the same horror we rightly feel reading about slavery in the history books.

Real progress means respecting the inalienable rights of every human being, no matter how small and defenseless. It means empowering women with real options, real health care, real choice. And it means throwing *Roe* onto the ash heap of history *where it belongs*.

What to Say When Abortion Supporters Say We Need to Codify *Roe V. Wade*:

- Only a half-dozen countries—including China and North Korea—have a national law as barbaric as *Roe*. There's no reason to bring it back.
- Proposals to codify *Roe* usually are far more extreme than even *Roe* was.

- Most who support codifying *Roe* don't know what *Roe* allowed. Ask them what abortion regulations codifying *Roe* would allow.
- Real progress means respecting the rights of all human beings—born and unborn.

CHAPTER 7
In Their Own Words

It is better to remain silent at the risk of being thought a fool,
than to talk and remove all doubt of it.

—Maurice Switzer, Author[1]

Teenagers Brooke Alexander and Billy High had been dating for just a few months. But a late-summer pregnancy test in 2021 changed everything.[2]

Brooke wanted an abortion. But the Texas Heartbeat Act, which protects unborn children from abortion once a heartbeat can be detected, was just about to take effect, so she'd need to get a quick ultrasound to find out whether she was past the cutoff point. Brooke mistakenly wound up at a pro-life pregnancy center, where an ultrasound revealed she was pregnant . . .

. . . with twins.

The sight of twins would seem to double the motivation for having an abortion. Double diapers. Double midnight feedings. Double *everything*.

Instead, the ultrasound reminded Brooke—and her mother—of the humanity of the babies she carried. "Oh, my God, oh my God— This is a miracle from the Lord," Brooke's mom said. "We are having these babies."[3] Brooke, too, was inspired by the twin heartbeats not to travel out of state for an abortion. She chose life and married Billy.

The *Washington Post* first reported on Brooke and Billy just days before the Supreme Court overturned *Roe*, lamenting that the Texas Heartbeat Act prevented them from getting an abortion. A little more than a year later, the *Washington Post* checked in with them again—and made sure readers know their lives would have been much better had they gotten an abortion instead of their two beautiful little girls.

"Sitting on the edge of her bed, hair dripping wet, the 19-year-old listened to her twin daughters cry in their high chairs on the other side of the door," read the second article. "One hurled what sounded like a plate. Then a bottle."[4] The piece—ominously titled, "An abortion ban made them teen parents"—features photos depicting all the chaos and disorder that come with raising twin toddlers.[5]

It's not always a pretty picture. As teen parents, Brooke and Billy have struggled with their marriage. They've struggled with finances. They argue about how much time Billy spends playing video games. The *Washington Post* articles create the impression that Billy is lazy and unhelpful while Brooke is shrill and jealous. Readers are left to consider whether the overturning of *Roe* will only serve to multiply the hardship of couples like Brooke and Billy. "[W]omen who are denied abortions experience worse financial, health, and family outcomes than those who are able to end their pregnancies,"[6] the article alleged, citing an admittedly pro-abortion study filled with dramatic methodological errors.[7]

Talking points like this are nothing new. What *is* new is the transition from abstract claims about the benefits of abortion to suggestions that perhaps *specific* babies should have been aborted. The *Washington Post* articles certainly hint that maybe everybody would be better off if Texas had just allowed Brooke to abort her twins: "The Texas law [that prevented Brooke from getting an abortion made] Brooke and Billy an early example of a family compelled into existence by an abortion ban."[8]

Just like that, the *Washington Post* was no longer weighing and bartering the value of nameless, faceless *fetuses*. It was weighing and bartering the value of *Kendall and Olivia High*.

This sort of rhetoric is cold and callous. But it's good for pro-lifers because it shows how out of touch abortion advocates are. Normal, healthy, functioning adults just don't look at Kendall and Olivia as *the abortions that could have been*. They see a pair of adorable, if rambunctious, little girls.

They also see that Kendall and Olivia haven't exactly ruined Brooke's and Billy's lives. The *Washington Post* article closed with Brooke, a high school dropout,[9] excitedly working with a career coach as she considered becoming a certified personal trainer and nutritionist. Meanwhile, the twins prompted Billy to leave a job at a burrito restaurant and to serve his country in the U.S. Air Force. And while they haven't made any decisions yet, the two are considering having another child.[10] Perhaps parenting hasn't been that bad after all!

For better *and* for worse, abortion supporters have grown increasingly unhinged since the Supreme Court's decision to overturn *Roe*. Share these disturbing quotations to show just how disconnected abortion advocates are from basic human decency.

Don't take our word for it; let's explore—and be equipped to share—their responses:

"The fact that things like inflation can happen and it can become more expensive to feed your kids and to fuel your car

is exactly why people need to be able to be in charge of how many mouths they're going to have to feed."
—*U.S. Rep. Katie Porter*[11]

With inflation running rampant in 2022, Representative Porter appeared to propose a novel solution for families struggling with inflation: just kill the unborn children who are too expensive to provide for.

"I would like to find out who [leaked the Supreme Court case ruling], so I could make sweet love to that person, because that person is a hero to me. . . . And if the leaker . . . is a Republican, and if I get pregnant during our lovemaking, I will joyfully abort our fetus, and let them know."
—*Emmy-nominated writer, comedian, and* New York Times *best-selling author Laurie Kilmartin*[12]

Abortion advocates used to justify the choice to kill an unborn child as a complex, personal, and difficult decision a woman makes only after thoughtful consideration. Kilmartin's shocking remarks on MSNBC suggest otherwise. The good news is her rant will not resonate at all with the women struggling over how to respond to an unexpected pregnancy.

"Misoprostol is relatively easy to acquire from veterinary sources, since in addition to medically inducing abortions, it's also used to treat ulcers in horses."
—*Motherboard/Tech by Vice*[13]

It wasn't long ago when abortion advocates warned of the dangers of back-alley abortions. But when the Supreme Court's decision to overturn *Roe* was leaked to *Politico*, Vice showcased an "anarchist collective" video instructing women how to make do-it-yourself abortion pills at home using drugs meant for farm animals.[14]

"*Dobbs* forced at least 1,500 unintended births, causing harm to Wisconsin communities. . . . *Dobbs* meant that during the first half of 2023, at least 1,503 people . . . were forced into carrying pregnancies to term that they would not have if abortion were more accessible. Why does this matter? It matters because science tells us that individuals, families and communities are harmed in many ways by restricting people's ability to access abortion."
    —*University of Wisconsin-Madison professors Tiffany Green and Jenny Higgins*[15]

The birth of a child is usually considered a good thing—but apparently not to University of Wisconsin professors Green and Higgins. And the most problematic of these births were those of "people of color" and "low-income Wisconsinites."[16] *It's science.*

"Women who are poor, women of color . . . will be forced to have pregnancies that they cannot afford to terminate, and pregnancies that will then turn into children."
    —*NBC News correspondent Yamiche Alcindor*[17]

Green and Higgins weren't alone in lamenting the number of minority babies who would survive pregnancy after *Dobbs*.

"In a time when we are experiencing more intense, disruptive climate impacts, the consequences of this Supreme Court decision will be even more harmful and deadly, with Black people and low-income people bearing the worst. . . . Climate change also puts stress on the ability of abortion clinics, which struggle to meet demands even during normal times."
    —*National Resources Defense Council national policy director and senior attorney Valerie Baron*[18]

They are *really* worried about black people and poor people having babies—especially in bad weather.

"[T]oday's decision [*Dobbs*] calls into question other rights that we thought were settled, such as . . . the right to interracial marriage."
—*Vice-President Kamala Harris*[19]

Even as abortion advocates push to abort more black babies, they allege that legally protecting unborn babies creates a slippery slope toward banning interracial marriage. They didn't, however, provide an explanation of why black pro-life Supreme Court Justice Clarence Thomas would seek to ban . . . *his own marriage*.

Even as religious belief and practice declines throughout the West, nearly two-thirds of American adults consider themselves to be Christians.[20] That means—as hostile as the abortion industry is toward Christianity—Planned Parenthood and its friends still need to market their product to believers.

"[W]omen in my congregation . . . are struggling with these choices, whether it's genetic abnormalities of fetuses, or just really struggling to understand—*What is life, and how does God produce life? What is God's place in all of that?* [Some women] grew up really religiously conservative and are saying, 'Am I going to go to hell for making this decision? What does the Bible say?' To be able to offer them a different answer, using my religious authority, is a gift."
—*Presbyterian pastor Jessie Commeret*[21]

Commeret is part of a post-*Roe* boom in pro-choice clergy—activists masquerading as ministers to hawk abortion. "Across the U.S., as state legislatures restrict reproductive health care in increasingly draconian ways, progressive faith communities are pushing back," writes Christina Cauterucci in *Slate*. "In Ohio, Christian ministers are learning how to safely terminate pregnancies at home. In Texas, pastors are boarding planes with groups of pregnant women and accompanying them to abortion clinics out of state. In Washington, D.C., a century-old Jewish nonprofit is shifting hundreds of thousands of dollars to abortion funds."[22]

"If abortions aren't safe than [sic] neither are you."
  —*Jane's Revenge*[23]

The shadowy pro-abortion movement "Jane's Revenge" wreaked havoc on pro-life organizations following the overturning of *Roe*—including a cyberattack on 40 Days for Life. Some attacks included this threat. It should come as no surprise that those who champion violence as a solution to a challenging pregnancy use violence to advance their political objectives as well.

"[M]ore of this. May these people never know a moment of peace or safety until they rot in the ground."
  —*Rewire News Group reporter Caroline Reilly in response to the firebombing of a pro-life organization*[24]

Abortion supporters like to paint pro-lifers as extremists, but more than 100 pro-life pregnancy centers and churches were attacked with violence and vandalism in the months following the leak that *Roe* would be overturned.[25] The targeting of pregnancy centers was particularly ironic, as the same people who argue pro-lifers "only care about babies until they're born" ransacked the very charities that support babies and empower moms *years* after birth.

"None of us should accept a future in which our daughters and granddaughters have fewer rights than we did."
   —*Former first lady, U.S. senator, and Secretary of State Hillary Clinton*[26]

Speaking of irony, Secretary Clinton failed to note that the daughters and granddaughters whose babies are now protected by the law are only alive today because they *themselves* were not aborted.

"I mean, so the idea that we're going to make a judgment that is going to say that no one can make the judgment to choose to abort a child based on a decision by the Supreme Court, I think, goes way overboard."
   —*President Joe Biden*[27]

If you skim it, this looks like just another meandering quote from a president whose age has clearly caught up with him. But if you read closely, President Biden acknowledges that *Roe* doesn't just abort a pregnancy. It aborts a *child.* Good one, Joe; we'll take what we can get.

"Restricting access to abortion does not prevent people from seeking abortion; it only makes it more deadly."
   —*Stephane Dujarric, spokesman for United Nations Secretary-General Antonio Guterres*[28]

MORE deadly?
President Biden wasn't the only pro-abortion world leader to respond to *Dobbs* with a Freudian slip.

"A big, hearty 'f—— you' to everyone who said I was overreacting by saying this could happen."
   —*Planned Parenthood senior director of news content*[29] *Kate Smith*[30]

At least we get honesty here. A little obscenity from Planned Parenthood seemed likely after the Supreme Court was about to overturn *Roe*. What's interesting about Kate Smith is she had been a supposedly objective "abortion access" reporter for CBS prior to stepping down so she could drop the mask and openly advocate for abortion. "Now that I'm not a reporter I can be candid about my own opinions on reproductive rights," she wrote.[31]

Smith's reaction to *Dobbs* illustrates why Americans increasingly distrust mainstream media. Her views on the issue weren't exactly hard to decipher even before her career change. "She is Planned Parenthood's ambassador to CBS, posing as a reporter and constructing articles that more closely resemble press releases for the nation's most powerful abortion-rights advocacy groups," wrote *National Review*'s Alexandra DeSanctis. "She has traded her objectivity for access to these organizations, offering them the kid-glove treatment so they will permit her to be the first to publicize their PR campaigns, interview their leaders, and scoop their briefs in court cases."[32]

❧

Don't be afraid of being labeled an "extremist" or a "Christian nationalist" for recognizing the dignity of human life. Instead, let abortion supporters' own words demonstrate which side of the abortion debate has actually lost touch with reality.

What to Say:

- Abortion advocates didn't address science or the legal proceedings overturning *Roe*.
- Most reactions from abortion advocates were extreme, vulgar, threatening, perverted, or discriminatory.
- Calling for violence against a group of people they disagree with is never appropriate.

CHAPTER 8

Drive-Through Abortions

*Medicine . . . does not consist of compounding pills
and plasters; it deals with the very processes of life,
which must be understood before they may be guided.*

—Paracelsus[1]

Six months after *Roe v. Wade* was overturned, the abortion lobby struck back, as President Joe Biden's Food and Drug Administration took the unprecedented step of authorizing retail pharmacies to begin distributing abortion pills.[2]

Walgreens and CVS quickly announced plans to sell the pills,[3] which led to your friendly corner pharmacies supplanting Planned Parenthood as America's leading abortion providers. Morally *and* financially) bankrupt Rite Aid soon did the same.[4] The three chains—along with a number of smaller pharmacies across the United States—spent much of 2023 completing a certification process, with the first pharmacies distributing abortion pills later that year.[5]

Deregulating the abortion industry seemed like a misplaced priority for the FDA, especially as the country continued to reel in the wake of the post-COVID supply chain crisis. The Biden administration floundered in its response to the 2022–23 baby formula shortage that subjected half of formula-fed infants to unsafe feeding practices.[6] But at least it provided for one-stop shopping when it came to buying abortion pills. "Honey, when you get your abortion pill, can you grab me a Snickers bar and a Mountain Dew?"

The term *abortion pill* can be a little confusing because pill-induced abortions typically involve a two-drug cocktail that ends the life of a growing child[7] during the first trimester of pregnancy.

The first pill, mifepristone (RU-486), blocks the pregnancy-sustaining hormone progesterone, which is essential for an unborn child to develop.[8] Prior to the FDA decision expanding abortion pill access, mifepristone was only available directly from medical providers—or in some states via telemedicine.[9]

A second pill often used to prevent ulcers,[10] misoprostol, causes the uterus to contract and expels the baby.[11] Misoprostol was already dispensed in pharmacies prior to the FDA's move to expand mifepristone access.[12]

Pill-induced abortions are often referred to as "medication abortions," but the phrase is a misnomer. Medicine restores and preserves the healthy functioning of the human body. Abortion pills *break* a woman's healthy reproductive system, using chemicals to kill her developing child.

Nor do abortion pills prevent a woman from becoming a mother. The moment she conceives, she becomes the mother of a new, distinct, and unique human being. From this point on, her child is growing, moving, and processing nutrition. By the time a woman takes an abortion pill, her child's heart is already beating! Abortion pills aren't designed to prevent motherhood. They're designed to make a woman the mother of a dead child.

The FDA first approved mifepristone (mifeprex) as an abortion drug in 2000.[13] It took time for the pill to catch on. In 2001, chemical abortions accounted for only 6 percent of all pregnancy terminations. Ten years later, fewer than a quarter of all abortions were induced by pills. But throughout mifepristone's second decade on the market, abortion pill use grew dramatically until abortion pills became responsible for the majority of all abortions in 2020.[14]

What's responsible for the shift? For starters, a collapse in the market for abortion. The number of U.S. pregnancy terminations peaked in 1990 at more than 1.6 million abortions. By 2017, the number was cut almost in half.[15] The abortion industry saw the convenience of pill-induced abortions as a way to reverse the decades-long trend. "Killing a child in the womb no longer requires traveling to an abortion clinic, but can be accomplished without even leaving home," wrote Heritage Foundation senior legal fellow Thomas Jipping and Heritage Foundation Young Leaders Program member Isaac Bock.[16]

The convenience factor explains the drive to roll out retail pharmacy abortions, webcam/telemedicine abortions, and even *mail-order abortions*. And it's responsible for helping to reverse the downward trend in abortion numbers. After a nearly three-decade running decline, the number of abortions in the United States increased by 9 percent from 2017 to 2021.[17]

But that's not the only incentive for the abortion industry to steer women toward abortion pills. Chemical abortion is also more lucrative than surgical abortion because handing a woman a pill requires a lot less overhead than performing a surgery. Margins are high, as abortion providers acquire abortion pills for less than $100[18] and resell them for more than $500—making abortion pills a nine-figure market.[19] And while webcam and mail-order abortions (as well as the introduction of a generic abortion pill to the market[20]) lower abortion providers' costs, the savings aren't passed on to the consumer. A University of California San Francisco-based research program found the customer's cost for abortion pills increased by 13 percent between 2017 and 2020.[21]

Certainly, the moguls who backed the abortion pill's development are making bank. The progressive magazine *Mother Jones* cited court filings showing a "small group of investors" have pocketed tens of millions of dollars from their stake in bringing mifepristone to market.[22] "Their story has a dizzying plot that involves Cayman Islands shell companies, LLCs named after racehorses, a shadowy [and, it turns out, fictional] priest, a disbarred attorney, and a finance whiz behind an infamous Wall Street hedge fund collapse," wrote *Mother Jones* reporter Hannah Levintova.[23]

It's hard to blame the abortion industry for its reliance on slogans and euphemisms. "Abortion is a private matter between a woman and her doctor" is quite a bit more marketable than "Abortion is a private equity matter between a woman and her Cayman Islands-based shell company."

Abortion pills are undoubtedly the greatest threat to unborn babies and their mothers in the post-*Roe* world. Remember these three points whenever someone suggests abortion pills provide a safe, legal way for a woman to end an unwanted pregnancy.

Point 1: Abortion Pills Are Messy, Painful, and Dangerous

Planned Parenthood has long promoted pill-induced abortions by claiming they "may feel more natural, like a miscarriage."[24] But if you or someone you love has suffered a miscarriage, it's difficult to imagine the degree of tone-deafness required for Planned Parenthood's marketing department to suggest the tragedy of miscarriage as a selling point.

Planned Parenthood has also described chemical abortion as "nothing worse than a heavy period."[25] This isn't quite how the abortion giant's former employee of the year, Abby Johnson, described her abortion pill experience. "I sat there for hours bleeding, throwing up into the bathroom trashcan, crying, and sweating," she said, adding she felt like she was "sitting in the middle of a crime scene."[26]

Abby isn't alone. According to the Mayo Clinic, women might need painkillers after taking abortion pills, and they might not be able to "go about [their] usual daily routine" after a chemical abortion.[27] This was certainly the case for one woman who recalled, "I was amply prepared for the bleeding, but not for the pain. [I] spent a few hours in enough pain to be incoherent."[28]

But pill-induced abortions aren't just messy and painful. They're also dangerous. Abortion pill complications include hemorrhage, infection, isoimmunization, and death.[29] The Mayo Clinic advises women who take the abortion pill to have "access to emergency services."[30] And the abortion pill poses particularly grave risks to women carrying undiagnosed ectopic pregnancies[31]—especially when the deregulation of chemical abortions means women are increasingly getting abortion pills without a physical examination to provide such a diagnosis.

While abortion advocates claim abortion pills are safer than Tylenol, board-certified OB-GYN Dr. Ingrid Skop said the comparison is dishonest. "They look at the number of Americans who die of Tylenol overdoses, which is about 600 a year, and they compare it to the vastly undercounted deaths attributed to abortion."[32] But Skop said about 1 in 20 women who take abortion pills visit the emergency room, and 1 in 20 require surgery.[33]

According to the Charlotte Lozier Institute, one reason abortion pill complications go underreported is abortion providers tell women that if something goes wrong after the abortion, they should claim they are suffering a miscarriage—a dangerous lie that significantly increases the risk of multiple hospitalizations and follow-up surgery.[34]

Another woman who took abortion pills described her chemical abortion as "the most painful experience I've ever had in my life. . . . I literally said to my boyfriend . . . 'I just want to die.'"[35] Fortunately for her, that wish did not come true. But dozens of women *have* died after taking abortion pills.[36] In fact, despite not having any laws regulating abortion whatsoever, Canada didn't approve mifepristone for sale until 2015.[37] A woman died of septic shock—a known potential complication of mifepristone—during a 2001 clinical trial.[38]

And yet progressive cities like San Francisco, which imposes heavy restrictions on Happy Meals handed out to kids through the McDonald's drive-through window,[39] celebrate pharmacies handing out abortion pills to kids through the drive-through window. All in the name of public health.

Point 2: Widespread Availability of Abortion Drugs Makes Their Abuse and Misuse Inevitable

Expanding access to abortion pills is like playing with a loaded gun.

In 2019, Timika Thomas was pregnant with twins conceived via in vitro fertilization* when she picked up a prescription for progesterone from CVS. But the pharmacy

---

* The in vitro fertilization process is morally problematic, but we share this example to highlight the dangers of widespread abortion drugs.

mistakenly gave her misoprostol pills instead. Thomas ended up losing the twins.[40]

While there's no way to determine definitively whether the misoprostol directly ended the lives of her embryos or whether the in vitro process simply failed,[41] Thomas believed the error took the lives of her children. *They killed my babies*, she thought upon realizing the mistake.[42] The tragic story illustrates the dangers of proliferating abortion drugs. "[P]eople make mistakes," Thomas acknowledged. "[But] that mistake took something from me."[43]

Both mifepristone and misoprostol have legitimate uses managing nonpregnancy-related conditions like Cushing syndrome and rheumatoid arthritis. This is why—contrary to the fearmongering of abortion advocates[44]—pro-lifers aren't trying to *ban* the drugs. We're trying to make sure the drugs are used to heal, not to kill. When the misuse or abuse of a medication has deadly consequences, tight control over the drug's availability is appropriate. "There's not enough therapy," Thomas said. "There's not enough medication that'll take the thoughts away. That will take the pain away."[45]

The error that cost Thomas her twins was a mistake, but widespread availability of abortion pills also puts a target on the backs of women who *want* their babies. One in four women who have had abortions report the terminations were unwanted or coerced.[46] And the danger is particularly acute among the most vulnerable women.

"This injustice [of coerced abortion] is especially common among women enslaved in sex trafficking," wrote a panel of Charlotte Lozier Institute researchers. "Clearly, over-the-counter access to mifepristone [a goal abortion advocates are pursuing[47]] would make it easier for sex traffickers and sexual predators to instigate and oversee the coerced abortions of their victims while eliminating any risk that crimes might be revealed and reported by health care providers."[48]

Other efforts to expand the availability of abortion drugs carry the same risk. "The FDA's recent approval of mail-order abortions only increases this danger," wrote David C. Reardon, director of the Elliot Institute and associate scholar at the Charlotte Lozier Institute. "Now, anyone can obtain and stockpile abortion pills for use against women who refuse to abort voluntarily."[49]

Reardon's concern isn't hypothetical:

- A Florida man switched the label on a bottle of antibiotics, tricking his pregnant girlfriend into ingesting an abortion drug, which induced an unwanted abortion.[50]
- An Arlington, Virginia, doctor put an abortion pill in his girlfriend's tea, killing their baby at 17 weeks' gestation.[51]
- A Wisconsin man slipped a mifepristone pill into his girlfriend's smoothie. She became suspicious and had the beverage tested. A lab revealed the smoothie contained the abortion drug. The perpetrator fled the country before being arrested a decade later.[52]
- A Japanese man was charged after he told his teenaged girlfriend that he might have infected her with a sexually transmitted disease and gave her abortion pills under the guise they were meant to treat the feigned infection.[53]
- A 15-month investigation led to the arrest of a New York man charged with administering mifepristone to a pregnant woman without her knowledge, inducing an abortion.[54]
- A Texas man was indicted after his wife accused him of "lecturing her . . . on the importance of hydration

during pregnancy" and giving her a glass of water with the abortion pill mixed into it. The husband tried to claim the water was cloudy due to "dirty pipes."[55]

That's just a sampling of the cases where women were tricked or almost tricked into ingesting abortion drugs. How many more moms and babies will be hurt as abortion pills flood pharmacies? And mailboxes? And as physicians prescribe abortion pills to women who aren't even pregnant, so they can stock the drugs in their medicine cabinet for a rainy day?[56]

Point 3: If a Woman Takes the First Abortion Pill, It's Not Too Late to Save Her Baby

While the use of abortion pills has exploded in recent years, there is good news: Unlike a surgical abortion, chemical abortions can often be reversed provided a woman acts quickly after taking the mifepristone pill.[57]

Remember that the first abortion pill, mifepristone, blocks the hormone progesterone, which is necessary to sustain pregnancy. Abortion pill reversal (APR) provides a high dose of progesterone to overwhelm the mifepristone. "With so many medications, you can call poison control, and there's an antidote for it," OB-GYN and 40 Days for Life vigil campaign leader Dr. Monique Ruberu said. "This is the antidote to mifepristone."[58]

Ruberu's 40 Days for Life vigil in front of a Philadelphia abortion facility has helped numerous moms save their babies after taking the first abortion pill. In one case, she played a role in nearly every step of the abortion-vulnerable child's journey into the world, as she directed the mother to APR while standing vigil, personally administered the APR protocol, and was even on duty to assist with the delivery![59]

"Think of a hormone as a key that turns a lock and allows a door to open," explained Dr. George Delgado, who pioneered APR. "Mifepristone, being a receptor blocker, is like a false key. It fits into the lock but does not turn the lock to open the door."[60] But a high dose of progesterone can overwhelm the ability of the mifepristone to fill all the hormone receptors. "Instead of just one true key and one false key, you have multiple true keys outnumbering the false keys," Dr. Delgado continued. "That would give the good guys an advantage in the competition to enter the lock. The more times the good keys enter the lock, the better the chances of defeating the false keys."[61]

The science is interesting, but does APR actually work? There are no guarantees for any individual case, but studies indicate APR succeeds at saving the unborn child's life about two-thirds of the time. The protocol has saved thousands of babies[62] and is most effective when administered as soon as possible after the mifepristone dose is taken. Furthermore, progesterone is a naturally occurring hormone[63], which Dr. Delgado noted has long been used during pregnancy *safely*.[64]

Abortion advocates looking to discredit APR cite a pro-abortion study comprising only 10 women who took mifepristone to terminate a pregnancy. Half of the women then went through the APR protocol, while half received a placebo. When 3 of the 10 women developed bleeding complications and went to the emergency room, the study came to an abrupt end.[65]

Abortion advocates pounced on the study's early termination, proclaiming "not completing the abortion pill regimen can be life-threatening."[66] But even setting aside the fact a study of just 10 women provides a laughably small sample size, abortion advocates also ignore that two of the three women who experienced complications didn't receive APR but the placebo. Both required emergency D&C procedures, and one needed a blood transfusion. The only subject who experienced complications after actually completing the APR protocol did not require any treatment.[67]

APR is also safe for babies. Progesterone has long been used to help sustain at-risk pregnancies. Furthermore, according to the American Academy of Obstetricians and Gynecologists, there is no evidence that progesterone has harmful effects on an unborn child.[68] Initial studies show no increase in the birth defect rate after APR.[69]

If you or someone you know is looking to reverse an abortion, don't wait. Call 877-558-0333 or visit abortionpill reversal.com to find a medical professional who can help.

What to Say When the Abortion Pill Comes Up:

- Chemical abortions are messy, painful, and dangerous.
- Flooding communities with abortion pills is a recipe for disaster.
- Pill-induced abortions can be reversed.

CHAPTER 9

Men Can Get Abortions

My psychiatrist told me I was crazy and I said
I want a second opinion. He said okay, you're ugly too.
—Rodney Dangerfield[1]

What to Say When Someone Claims Men Can Get Pregnant:

- No, they can't.
- Men have never been able to get pregnant.
- Men will never be able to get pregnant.

CHAPTER 10

The Destruction of Women

It's worth it and it's necessary, so bring it on.
Bring on the men in dresses. There's a lot of things that scare me,
but a man in a dress will never be one of them.

—Riley Gaines, Women's Sports Advocate,
12x All-American Swimmer, 5X SEC Champion[1]

Okay, we'll go a little deeper than the previous chapter. When discussing the transgender craze and abortion, less is often more. But the alliance of the trans movement and the pro-abortion movement has become so aggressive that we can't avoid talking about it (as much as we might like to).

At first glance, the abortion and LGBTQ issues appear unrelated. Same-sex relationships are sterile and can't result in pregnancy. But the homosexual movement has actively inserted itself into the abortion debate because both the trans and pro-abortion movements are built on a shared philosophy: sexual license that accepts no sexual limitations from church, state, or culture. Both abortion advocates and homosexual advocates alike generally believe sex should be free for any reason, with anyone, and with zero consequences. And they demand that this philosophy be accepted by *everyone*. The two movements are locked arm in arm not only in principle but also financially. This is why you see so many Pride flags at pro-abortion events and abortion rights signs at Pride parades.

Enter the transgender movement. Homosexual activists achieved total victory in 2015 when the Supreme Court forced all 50 states to legally recognize same-sex relationships as marriages. But the revolution never ends—it just finds a new outlet for upending society. So it's no surprise that the same year, the TQ (transgender/queer) end of the LGBTQ acronym rose to prominence as Olympic legend Bruce Jenner insisted he is a woman named "Caitlyn."

Just like the homosexual cause, the trans movement has joined forces with the pro-abortion movement. Abortion appears to be next, as trans advocates shout, "Trans men are men . . . and sometimes they need abortions!" We are reaching peak insanity.

The pendulum may well swing back toward sanity sooner rather than later because the coalition of sexual deviants supporting the abortion industry becomes increasingly unstable. The abortion industry has long been allied with a feminist movement built on advancing the interests of women. But now the abortion industry has joined forces with a trans movement that essentially denies there is such a thing as a woman. Increasingly bizarre rhetoric reveals that the abortion industry/radical feminism/LGBTQ unholy trinity is built on a house of cards. And it's on the brink of collapse.

Perhaps no two movements in the history of the world have put more emphasis on the reality of biological sex than feminists and homosexuals.

For more than a century, feminists have worked for equality in the workplace, equality in sports, and celebration of the many things women can do as well as or better than men. This approach is well intentioned—even if it sometimes seriously goes off the rails by veering into advocacy for abortion and other evils. But whether the feminist movement is right or wrong on a given issue, it's indisputably true that for feminists *being a woman matters.* The difference between women and men matters. Your sex was no more "assigned at birth" than the reproductive organs you have. Vaginas and penises are not interchangeable to feminists. They are absolutely binary, and they are relevant to feminists and to their cause.

Men cannot get pregnant. Men don't bear the joys and pains of pregnancy, labor, and delivery. Men do not make the sacrifices necessary to breastfeed their children. The feminists know this as well as anyone, and they have traditionally been the loudest in sharing it.

The homosexual movement, too, understands that "biological sex" is a redundant term. This is why the LGBTQ movement was always destined to fracture. On one hand, you've got the "TQ" side of the acronym that argues an infinite number of genders exist, genders can change, or there's no such thing as gender. On the other hand, the "LG" side of the acronym takes the reality of biological sex so seriously that homosexual people choose their sexual partners based on the reality of their biological sex.

Homosexual men want to have sex with other men *because* they're men. Lesbians want to have sex with women *because* they're women. Homosexual people often go so far as to root their very identity in their attraction to the same sex. They dedicate an entire month to celebrating their attraction to members of the same sex. They spent decades pushing for legal and social recognition of *same-sex* marriage.

Christians and homosexual activists sharply disagree on the morality of sexual relationships between two individuals of the same sex. But we can at least agree on what those relationships *are* and who they involve.

Transgender activists throw that shared understanding—which has been in place for all of human history—right out the window. Some insist that gay men must actually be straight trans women. Others insist that lesbians are bigots if they refuse to date trans women (who are actually men).

The previous paragraph would be laughable—if it wasn't the dominating philosophy in media, politics, business, entertainment, and academia. But the bottom line is, the transgender movement is driving a wedge between itself and some of the other progressive movements you probably think of as their natural allies: the feminist and homosexual movements.

They don't always admit it publicly, but many feminists and homosexuals are outraged at how the trans movement has hijacked their causes. We got a peek at this when there were split opinions on whether trans women (actual men) could be part of the Women's March. These types of divisions show why the alliance between feminism and transgenderism is not sustainable.

Remember these three points when transgender nonsense enters your discussion on abortion:

Point 1: There Are Only Two Sexes— and You Can't Change from One to Another

You're not crazy. Men cannot be women and women cannot be men. There are two sexes—always have been and always will be. No medication or surgery can change this reality.

To affirm those suffering gender dysphoria is to participate in a lie. We cannot participate in the lie no matter how loudly and forcefully transgender advocates shout. If I demand that you call me a woman (or address me as Frank

Sinatra or Rosa Parks or President Ulysses S. Grant), you should not acquiesce.

It would be easy to just disregard transgender activists because we don't want to deal with them and think they're crazy. But that's a lazy, disrespectful, and irresponsible approach. Even though we know their agenda is insane, we must always remember this: trans ideology has real victims.

At the same time, the transgender craze has evolved from a small group of people who genuinely suffer from gender dysphoria and need our compassion into a cultural fad that thrives on narcissism. This fad is a means to become the center of attention. When attempting to transition into the opposite sex is no longer novel enough for TikTok cred, just go ahead and invent a new designer gender. Failure to acknowledge made-up genders, names, and pronouns can get you labeled transphobic, and before you know it, you'll identify as *unemployed*.

The reality is that no one is transphobic because there is no such thing as transgender.

Trans advocates know this in their hearts, which is why they constantly repeat the slogan, "Trans women are real women." To paraphrase Shakespeare, "She/her doth protest too much, methinks." The "trans women are real women" mantra—like "abortion is health care"—is repeated ad nauseum precisely because everybody knows it's not true. If somebody gave you a $20 bill, insisting, "This is a *real* $20 bill," you'd immediately assume it's a counterfeit.

Can you imagine a feminist saying, "Working women are real women"? Or "Women athletes are real women"? They don't have to because those truths are obvious to all. Similarly, as pro-lifers we don't argue that "unborn babies are real babies." We make the case that "abortion kills a baby."

Whether they're suffering from real gender dysphoria or giving in to the latest pop culture trend, the trans lifestyle dehumanizes its victims by stripping them of their authentic dignity. The fact that this dehumanization is self-inflicted makes it all the sadder.

An increasingly diverse group of people including Riley Gaines, Bill Maher, Matt Walsh, Joe Rogan, and Dr. Paul McHugh point this out every day. And as early as 2015, McHugh, a Democrat, noted how dangerous the trans ideology is:

> The idea that one's sex is a feeling, not a fact, has permeated our culture and is leaving casualties in its wake. Gender dysphoria should be treated with psychotherapy, not surgery. Transgendered men do not become women, nor do transgendered women become men. All (including Bruce Jenner) become feminized men or masculinized women, counterfeits or impersonators of the sex with which they "identify." In that lies their problematic future.[2]

That problematic future is being imposed by those who insist that "transphobia" is violence. If we don't affirm one's gender delusions, the person will end his or her own life. In other words, "Give me what I want, or I'll kill myself." Trans advocates are taking *themselves* hostage. And if the hostages get killed, they accuse *you* of murder because you refused to indulge their fantasies.

Of course, it's all a lie. The sad reality is that the suicide rate of those who identify as trans and are *affirmed* in it is sky-high. "When 'the tumult and shouting dies,' it proves not easy nor wise to live in a counterfeit sexual garb," McHugh explained. "The most thorough follow-up of sex-reassigned people—extending over thirty years and conducted in Sweden, where the culture is strongly supportive of the trans-gendered—documents their lifelong mental unrest. Ten to fifteen years after surgical reassignment, the suicide rate of those who had undergone sex-reassignment surgery rose to twenty times that of comparable peers."[3]

Point 2: A "Trans Man" Is a Woman . . . and Men Cannot Have Abortions

The notion that men can get pregnant and have babies is the greatest insult to women of our lifetime.

And it's brand-new. Can you imagine Jane Fonda, Whoopi Goldberg, or Hillary Clinton, or any feminist from even 20 years ago saying, "Men can have babies"? But amazingly, some of the same feminists who championed abortion by arguing, "I'm a woman, not a womb," now reduce their identity to their reproductive capacity by self-identifying as "birthing persons."

Clearly the feminist movement has failed if women can no longer claim exclusive domain over the unique genius to conceive, bear, nourish, and nurture another human being. And if men can have babies, it was only a matter of time before we'd be told that men can have abortions.

Confused yet? You're not alone.

Presidential candidate Julian Castro said in a debate, "I don't believe only in reproductive freedom. I believe in reproductive justice. . . . Just because a woman—or let's also not forget someone in the trans community, a trans female—

is poor, doesn't mean they shouldn't have the right to exercise that right to choose."[4] Even *Politico* was confused with his response, "Hmm. Trans females needing access to abortion. Biologically speaking, when would that be necessary?"[5]

It's because "trans females" are men. Dudes, boys, jocks, meatheads, bros, muchachos—however you want to word it, they're men, and men can't have abortions. In his pandering, poor Castro apparently forgot what his own talking points mean. Who can blame him for getting confused? It's hard to redefine human existence.

If your head is spinning, too, don't worry; you haven't lost your mind. Rest assured, in the entire history of human existence, every "trans man" who claims to have gotten pregnant or had an abortion is a woman. She might pretend to be a man. She might dress up like a man. She might even believe herself to be a man. But she's a woman who was impregnated by a man.

Point 3: To Claim That Men Can Get Pregnant and Have Abortions Is Insulting to All Women

Women who have abortions—whether they regret it or not—know it was a serious and hard decision. The way abortion supporters discuss the topic, you'd get the impression that abortion is the Vince Lombardi trophy of what women can accomplish in post-*Roe* America. The staunchest and loudest abortion supporters have turned it into a sacrament.

In this brave new world, the essence of womanhood is access, willingness, and ability to get an abortion. Abortion is seen as the pinnacle of the female experience—socially, politically, and morally. There's just one problem: Real women don't agree.

After the *Dobbs v. Jackson Women's Health Organization* decision leaked, liberal comedian and pundit Bill Maher admitted he didn't realize that the majority of pro-life Americans are women.[6] Among abortion supporters, Bill Maher was lonely in his honesty. Pro-abortion celebrities, influencers, and politicians refused to accept anything less than abortion on-demand through all 40 weeks of pregnancy.

The exaltation of abortion as a trophy for women inevitably led "trans women" (men) to clamor to be the first biological male to get an abortion.

A trans activist who calls himself Rhiannon Rose appeared in a video, declaring:

> I want to be the first trans woman to have an abortion. I will let a doctor who has successfully transplanted a uterine complex before, cut the organs out of a willing, healthy, trans masculine donor, place them in my body. I will devote myself, heart and soul, to their aftercare. I will have as much gay sex as it takes with as many trans women as it takes, and let the transphobes and homophobes scratch their heads wondering what to make of it. And I want to be the first trans woman to have an abortion.[7]

It's also no longer about abortion. This man is a narcissist trying to get even more people to talk about him, his feelings, and what he wants.

It's incredibly insulting.

For the millions of women who have lain on the table and had an abortion—whether they regret it or not—abortion is serious. It's not a plea for attention or a charade to offend Christians. It is a difficult, lonely, and scary decision, the memory of which may never go away.

But the abortion-desiring trans activist is not thinking about women who've had abortions. He's thinking about himself and how he can generate clicks. He's literally just another man who could care less about women. He insults women by pretending to be one; he insults women by claiming he's entitled to pregnancy; and he insults them by trivializing abortion.

"There is . . . something in these desires that goes beyond the usual narcissism and wish-fulfillment of men calling themselves women," wrote Ann Furedi, who is no right-wing Christian. She's a former British abortion executive whom 40 Days for Life has debated on the radio. She continued: "They reveal a brutal and barbaric view of abortion that is almost never expressed by actual women. In my more than 20 years of providing abortion services . . . I have never met a single woman who said it was her ambition to abort a pregnancy."[8]

Attacking women in the name of women's rights is not something new. And it's not something we should fear in conversation. But the transgender attempt to annihilate women is just one more piece of evidence that the pro-life side is the side of science, reason, nature, compassion, medical alternatives, and—of course—women.

What to Say When Abortion and Transgender Ideology Collide:

- There are only two sexes. Being male or female is essential to abortion advocates and abortion opponents alike.
- A "trans man" is a woman. When a "trans man" has an abortion, it is a woman having an abortion, not a man. Men cannot have abortions.
- Women who have abortions—whether they regret it or not—know it was a serious and hard decision. To claim that men can get pregnant and have abortions is insulting to all women.

CHAPTER 11

Politically Botching Abortion

*I believe this government cannot endure, permanently half slave
and half free. I do not expect the Union to be dissolved—
I do not expect the house to fall—but I do expect it will cease
to be divided. It will become all one thing or all the other.*

— Abraham Lincoln, "House Divided Speech," 1858[1]

On New Year's Day in 1863, President Abraham Lincoln
issued the Emancipation Proclamation. With one stroke
of his pen, Honest Abe liberated enslaved persons across the
country, brought a swift end to hostilities between the North
and South, and ushered in an era of racial peace and harmony.

Well . . . not exactly. While the Emancipation Proclamation served as a significant turning point, the end of slavery
and the restoration of respect for all human beings regardless
of their skin color proved to be a much messier process.

Legally, the Emancipation Proclamation liberated only
enslaved persons in Confederate states. Practically, it liberated only the enslaved persons in Confederate territories
under Union control. And at the time the proclamation was
issued, the Civil War wasn't even halfway done. The United
States' deadliest war—which cost more American lives than
both world wars, the Vietnam War, and the Korean War *combined*[2]—raged on for two more years.

It took three constitutional amendments, a presidential assassination, and a century of discriminatory Jim Crow laws before black Americans achieved equal treatment under the law. And still today, the 2020 death of George Floyd and a summer of coast-to-coast riots that followed provide another painful reminder: more than 150 years after abolition, anger over slavery and casting America into hell for the sin of slavery are, unfortunately, alive and well.

It's tempting to point to specific laws, court cases, executive orders, and military battles as having decisively and definitively *ended* particular human rights injustices. But history is rarely this simple. The end of slavery brought about new and difficult problems for black Americans and their allies: poll taxes, predatory sharecropping, institutionalized segregation, and many more.

Of course, no abolitionist ever regretted ending slavery, regardless of the challenges that emerged in its wake. Instead, civil rights advocates recognized the eradication of slavery wasn't the end of their work; it was a first step.

The same is true with abortion. The *Dobbs v. Jackson Women's Health Organization* decision was never going to result in *happily ever after*. The overturning of *Roe v. Wade* was quickly followed by abortion sanctuary states, deregulation of abortion pills, and violence against pro-life pregnancy centers. With the *Dobbs* decision, the Supreme Court simply got out of the way so that the real work of ending abortion can begin.

But shockingly, not all who align themselves with the pro-life movement have matched the resolve of the heroes of the nineteenth- and twentieth-century civil rights movements. Many of the politicians elected to office thanks to pro-life voters appear reluctant—almost embarrassed—to be defined as pro-life in the post-*Roe* era. While civil rights advocates endured police dogs, fire hoses, beatings, and murders, a couple of tough elections led political candidates to scrub their pro-life stance from their campaign websites.[3]

In 2023, Republican Party operatives urged congressional candidates not just to keep quiet about abortion but to actively campaign *against* legislation that would protect unborn children from abortion.[4] A super PAC warned Republican senators that polling data suggested even the term "pro-life" might be problematic.[5]

"What intrigued me the most about the results was . . . that people see being pro-life as being against all abortions . . . at all levels," said Republican North Dakota senator Kevin Cramer.[6] Fewer than eight months after he was honored with North Dakota Right to Life's "Life Protector Award,"[7] it apparently came as a surprise to Senator Cramer that being pro-life means you can't kill *any* innocent human beings. With friends like this, who needs enemies?

Even President Donald Trump, who nominated three of the five justices who voted to overturn *Roe*, took aim at pro-lifers, describing a Florida law that protects unborn children once a heartbeat can be detected as "a terrible thing and a terrible mistake."[8]

There's no doubt we pro-lifers have our work cut out for us. Pro-abortion candidates and referenda have been successful early in the post-*Roe* era. But nothing could be more shortsighted than to let a couple of tough elections dampen pro-life resolve—especially on the heels of a Supreme Court victory 50 years in the making.

Remember these three points whenever someone suggests that protecting unborn children and their moms from abortion is a political loser.

Point 1: Give It Time

Americans tell Washington, DC, they want *change* all the time. But they don't mean it. Americans are much more comfortable with the status quo. This is particularly true with regard to abortion.

Consider the following results from Gallup polling on whether Americans consider themselves pro-life or pro-choice:

- In October 2000, pro-choice Americans outnumbered pro-life Americans by 2 percent. Four months later, that gap swelled to 17 percent. What happened? George W. Bush, who campaigned as a pro-lifer, was elected and took office.[9]
- In May 2008, pro-choicers outnumbered pro-lifers by 6 percent. That fall, hardline pro-abortion Barack Obama was elected president. By May 2009, the margin swung 15 percent as pro-lifers achieved their first-ever majority in the Gallup poll.[10]

What's going on here? Are millions of Americans routinely changing their minds about abortion? Probably not. Most likely, they are merely reacting against the possibility of change.

And the overturning of *Roe* was a big change. In May 2021, pro-choicers again held a two-point lead. A year later, just before a Supreme Court leak revealed that the overturning of *Roe* was imminent, that advantage ballooned to 16 percent with pro-life support cratering to levels not seen in nearly two decades.[11]

The massive shift in public opinion is responsible for pro-lifers' Election Day disappointments. But will it last? History says it won't. And in fact, there are already signs that post-*Dobbs* pro-abortion sentiment has crested. Gallup's 16-point pro-choice advantage in 2022 was cut in half within a year—before the first anniversary of the *Dobbs* decision.[12] An 8-percent advantage is still enough to make a difference at the ballot box. And it did in states that held elections in November 2023.

But as more time passes, more Americans will recognize that overturning *Roe* did not cause the sky to fall. Not one woman has died from lack of access to abortion. Not one has been investigated or arrested for suffering a miscarriage. Tens of thousands of babies who would have been aborted are bringing joy to their families' lives. All of these developments have the potential to reverse the abortion industry's short-term advantage in public opinion.

As long as we don't give up.

"The more we talk about abortion, the worse we're doing," said 2012 presidential candidate Mitt Romney following pro-life losses in November 2023 elections.[13] It wasn't the first time Senator Romney tried to steer away from abortion. In the closing weeks of his 2012 presidential campaign, the supposedly pro-life Romney attempted to secure the election by airing ads listing various situations in which he supports killing unborn children.[14]

Romney's political instincts were wrong then. His campaign predicted he'd defeat President Obama "decisively" and backed up the bravado by prematurely ordering a celebratory fireworks display shortly before getting trounced in an Electoral College landslide.[15]

And Romney's instincts are wrong now. Instead of taking advice from a twice-failed presidential candidate, pro-lifers should look to the other side of the culture war to learn how perseverance wins. It's hard to imagine now, but same-sex marriage advocates had lost 32 straight referenda before the tide began to turn in 2012.[16]

Throughout the long losing streak, liberals didn't call upon same-sex marriage advocates to go away. Progressives didn't insist that they settle for some consensus compromise like civil unions. Even as Republicans actively sought to place marriage referenda on the ballot to help drive up religious voter turnout for George W. Bush's reelection campaign in 2004, 43 of 48 Democratic senators (plus one Democrat-aligned independent) voted against a constitutional amendment defining marriage as a union of one man and one woman. The Democrats' presidential ticket of John Kerry and John Edwards dodged the vote.[17]

So same-sex marriage advocates went for broke. *And they got it.* Just three years after winning their first referendum, they achieved total victory as the Supreme Court redefined marriage for all 50 states. Less than a decade later, no meaningful political opposition to same-sex marriage even exists.

Of course, the juggernaut has kept rolling. The movement transitioned (pardon the pun) from redefining marriage to redefining biological sex. On the eve of the SCOTUS marriage decision, Bruce Jenner claimed to be a woman. Schools and children's libraries invited drag queens to hold obscene performances for kids. And you can now be canceled for affirming basic biological realities, which were common sense—spanning geography, history, and culture—only a few years ago.

The LGBTQ movement's success has been a disaster for humanity. But it does provide pro-lifers with a much-needed example that trends in public opinion can change quickly. "We disagreed with [same-sex marriage supporters'] objective," wrote the editors at *National Review*. "[B]ut their success serves as a reminder that a string of defeats at the ballot box is no reason to believe a cause is lost."[18]

Point 2: Compromising Is a Losing Game

Nothing is inevitable in the post-*Roe* world. Every potential outcome is on the table—from nationwide recognition of the personhood of the unborn child to a backslide into a national codification of *Roe* that legalizes abortion through all nine months of pregnancy for any reason.

This doomsday scenario is scary, but it might not be the most *dangerous* potential outcome. The most dangerous situation is for America to slip into some sort of compromise on abortion.

"Sure, we'll ban third-trimester abortions," voters might say. "They're messy and unpopular." (Even most Democrats want to limit abortion to the first six months of pregnancy.)[19] "Maybe we could ban sex-selective abortions and limit taxpayer funding of abortion," they continue. "As long as we have exceptions for rape and incest. And the life of the mother. And the health of the mother. Or if the child has a disability."

While there's no place for third-trimester abortion or sex-selective abortions, pursuing these low-hanging fruits at the expense of the 93 percent of abortions that take place in the first trimester[20] would be the hollowest of victories.

In 2022, Republican senator Lindsey Graham of South Carolina introduced a federal bill to limit abortion to the first 15 weeks of pregnancy with exceptions for rape, incest, and the life of the mother.[21] Prominent pro-life politicians voiced support for a 15-week abortion ban in 2023, including presidential candidates Vice-President Mike Pence,[22] South

Carolina senator Tim Scott,[23] Florida governor Ron DeSantis,[24] and Virginia governor Glenn Youngkin.[25]

In other words, the standard for what it means to be pro-life in post-*Roe* America is support for abortion laws that are even more liberal than those in progressive, post-Christian *Europe*. Ninety-four percent of European countries have abortion limits at or earlier than 15 weeks.[26] The limit in France and Spain is 14 weeks, while Belgium, Denmark, Finland, Germany, Ireland, Italy, Luxembourg,[27] and Switzerland[28] prohibit abortion after 12 weeks.

Certainly, it's better to protect babies after 15 weeks' gestation than not to. But when politicians refuse to stand up for the rights of abortion-vulnerable children prior to 15 weeks, there's no historical evidence to suggest any further progress will be made. Instead, the deadly compromise becomes entrenched. As long as the grisliest late-term abortions are prohibited, citizens accept the slaughter of first-trimester babies. The controversy of abortion is diminished—and the diminishment of pro-lifers' efficacy usually follows.

Or, to paraphrase Lincoln, America cannot remain half pro-abortion and half pro-life.[29] Any effort that barters human lives for political capital will *forever* remain a country that kills its own children on an industrial scale.

Besides, once you start to bargain away human lives, the deals get worse. Former South Carolina governor Nikki Haley became the poster child for how badly supposedly pro-life Republicans dealt with abortion after the overturning of *Roe*. She lacked even the fight to push for a 15-week ban. "We don't need to divide America over this issue anymore," she said at a 2023 presidential debate before suggesting an even more lukewarm compromise.[30] "Can't we all agree that we are not going to put a woman in jail or give her the death penalty if she gets an abortion?"[31]

What??? Have you ever heard of anyone advocating the death penalty for women or abortion doctors? It was a curious remark. Absurdity to the highest degree.

But it was also instructive. Pro-lifers can't expect politicians to lead the way when it comes to ending abortions. Grassroots pro-lifers will need to lead, dragging the politicians—kicking and screaming if that's what it takes—across the finish line.

Point 3: The Winning Formula: Principle Plus Competence

Over the past quarter century, Florida has been among the tightest of political swing states. In the state's 2010,[32] 2014,[33] and 2018[34] gubernatorial elections, the winner's margin of victory never exceeded 1.2 percent. Then in 2022—a year widely considered to be a disappointment for Republicans nationwide—GOP governor Ron DeSantis cruised to a 19-point victory.[35]

How did DeSantis avoid being swept out by the post-*Dobbs* backlash? First, he went on offense. Unlike the Republican politicians who backtracked or apologized for their pro-life position, DeSantis embraced it. "Florida will continue to defend its recently enacted pro-life reforms against state court challenges, will work to expand pro-life protections, and will stand for life by promoting adoption, foster care, and child welfare," he said in the wake of the *Dobbs* decision.[36]

Perhaps DeSantis was able to avoid groveling about agreeing "not to give [a woman] the death penalty if she gets an abortion" because he had already faced—and won—numerous culture war battles during his first term. He faced a nationwide backlash for signing a series of bills derided as "Don't Say Gay" laws, which kept sexually explicit and

LGBTQ indoctrinations out of classrooms. "We never did this through all of human history until like, what, two weeks ago?" DeSantis said regarding the use of preferred pronouns in schools. "We're not doing the pronoun Olympics in Florida. It's not happening here."[37]

Clearly, DeSantis's straight shooting on life and culture issues resonated with voters, including some who weren't traditional Republican voters. "I have been a registered Democrat my entire life, but when my daughter decided to abort my grandchild, something inside me changed," said one Florida voter. "I want a governor, like DeSantis, to stop this madness and protect the unborn."[38]

Pro-life politicians fear being branded as "extreme"— particularly when they don't support abortion exceptions for hard cases like rape, incest, and pregnant women facing life-threatening medical conditions. But U.S. senator Rand Paul of Kentucky turned the tables by pointing out that abortion advocates are never called out for their extremism. "[W]e always seem to have the debate [over] exemptions," Paul told a reporter.[39] "You go back and you ask [Democratic National Committee chair] Debbie Wasserman Schultz if she's OK with killing a seven-pound baby that is just not born yet. . . . When you get an answer from Debbie, come back to me."[40]

Trump followed Paul's formula in the final debate of the 2016 presidential campaign. "If you go with what Hillary is saying, in the ninth month, you can take the baby and rip the baby out of the womb of the mother just prior to the birth of the baby," he noted.[41]

Trump's straight talk might have won him the election. Just weeks before, Trump appeared a long shot. Pro-lifers— already skeptical of Trump due to his previous pro-abortion position and a long history of moral failings—might have been tempted to vote third-party or not to vote at all. Instead, Trump's clarity won pro-life voters over, paving the way for a historic upset on election night.

As important as it is to rally the base, even on a divisive issue like abortion, there's still room for persuasion. For example, a Vinea Research poll conducted by Students for Life of America revealed young people overwhelmingly support abortion for any reason at least through the first three months of pregnancy. But the same poll shows a majority of survey respondents favor banning abortion once they learn that an unborn child's heart begins beating only three weeks after conception.[42] Young people also oppose *Roe* upon learning it allowed abortion all nine months of pregnancy as well as sex-selection abortions.[43]

None of this means that persuading voters is easy. But it becomes a lot less difficult when pro-life principles are combined with effective governance. No scandals. No fixating on grievances from past elections. No political theater. No celebrity baggage. Just competence. As columnist Michael A. Cohen noted after the 2022 election, "[P]erhaps, voters just preferred the workhorse to the show horse. . . . [V]oters were more interested in competence and experience at the helm of state government rather than ideology and intense partisanship."[44]

DeSantis wasn't the only one to outperform his fellow Republicans in 2022. Republican governors Brian Kemp (Georgia), Greg Abbott (Texas), and Mike DeWine (Ohio) were all targeted for signing pro-life bills into law. But each of them cruised to reelection by avoiding unnecessary drama and doing their jobs.

The lesson of the GOP's few bright spots in the 2022 elections might have been best articulated by a Democrat. "Boring wins," said Wisconsin governor Tony Evers after dispatching his Republican opponent in a race that wasn't as close as expected.[45]

When Hurricane Ian cut off 9,000 residents of Florida's Pine Island from the mainland, the DeSantis administration repaired bridges and restored access in just three days.[46] "The response was excellent," said a Pine Island small business owner. "Things got done. I still remember the day that the [grocery store] trucks went by here. It gave you goose bumps."[47]

Hot-button issues dominate the headlines and the airwaves, but most voters are more concerned about having traversable roads they can drive to get to work. "I think people gave him a lot of credit for the way he handled the hurricane," said pollster Brad Coker. "He stood shoulder to shoulder with Biden, didn't turn it into a political game, he played governor the way he was supposed to. I think some Democrats may have peeled off after that."[48]

Even in tightly contested battleground states, staunch pro-life candidates can win—as long as they do a good job managing the less flashy parts of the job that impact voters' day-to-day lives.

What to Say When You're Told Pro-Life Protections for Unborn Children Are a Recipe for Electoral Failure:

- The backlash to the overturning of *Roe v. Wade* won't last.
- Compromising the lives of unborn children means lost elections and lost lives.
- Voters will support pro-life candidates as long as they govern effectively.

CHAPTER 12

Where Are All the Dead Women?

*We got tired of tripping over women in . . . public
bathrooms who were giving themselves abortions . . .
because there was nowhere safe, nowhere clean, nowhere to go.*

—Whoopi Goldberg, Actor and Talk Show Host
(after a leak revealed the Supreme Court
planned to overturn *Roe v. Wade*)[1]

It was never verified where in the world poor Whoopi was
using the bathroom.

In a well-known scene of the first *Mission Impossible* film,
Tom Cruise's character's entire crew has been killed. He frantically screams at another agent, "They're dead! They're all
dead!"[2]

It's just the opposite in post-*Roe* America when it comes to
women dying because they don't have access to abortion. You
can confidently and calmly say, "No one is dead." Awkwardly,
it seems many wish women were dying. Some abortion supporters get quite enthusiastic about discussing women dying.

The reality is, abortion cannot save your life, which is why
no woman has died as a result of *Roe* being overturned. This
is a good thing.

Compare the cultlike devotion to the belief that women
will die without abortion to what would happen if people lost

access to legitimate health care procedures that actually do save lives. Imagine if 20 states banned heart surgery. Would people die? The very next day. What about chemotherapy? Yes. Liver transplants? All goners.

Think about this. Abortion, the most common surgery in the world, is sold as lifesaving, yet pro-life laws in states across the U.S. have not caused a single death. It's one of the oldest but most popular tricks in the book: If you're losing an argument, don't bother reconsidering your position or articulating your case more clearly. Just insist that mere disagreement with your opinion will *literally kill people.*

And it's not just Whoopi. If you don't believe us, just turn on any political news talk show.

- Do you want to slightly tweak some unsustainable government program? People will die.
- Would you like to see changes to federal income tax brackets? People will die.
- Did you skip the plant-based meat substitute and have a cheeseburger for lunch? Our children and grandchildren will die.
- Don't want to wear a mask at the grocery store? Grandmas will die.

The best part of insisting that anybody who disagrees with you is a murderer is you don't even need any evidence it's true. Righteous indignation is enough—and the louder, the better.

Nobody has spent more time and energy perfecting this disingenuous debate tactic than the abortion industry, which has long asserted that *any* restriction on abortion will kill women.

The executive vice president of Planned Parenthood Federation of America, Dawn Laguens, claimed the Mexico City

policy (which denies federal funds to nongovernmental organizations that perform, refer for, and promote abortion) killed
approximately 70,000 women per year prior to President
Barack Obama repealing it in 2009.[3] When President Donald
Trump reinstated and expanded the policy after taking office
in 2017, the vice president for external relations for the international *faith-based* health care nonprofit organization IMA
World Health, Amy Gopp, alleged, "Women will die because
of this order."[4]

Population Action International director of advocacy
Jonathan Rucks blamed the Mexico City policy for eliminating funding for nongovernmental organizations that combat
HIV, malaria, and tuberculosis.[5] He should have blamed
the organizations themselves for prioritizing abortion over
actual health care. The U.S. government would have happily continued funding their work if only those organizations dropped their insistence on pushing abortion. Nearly
five years later, *the Mercury News* chimed in with an editorial
claiming "women will die as a result" of a 2021 Supreme
Court decision that upheld the Texas Heartbeat Act, which
effectively made abortion illegal in the Lone Star State six
weeks into pregnancy.[6]

And even though one of the abortion industry's favor-
ite slogans is "trust women," abortion advocates apparently
don't trust that women are capable of finding health care if
it doesn't come from Planned Parenthood. A 2015 article in
Forbes claimed that defunding Planned Parenthood would
endanger the lives of 900,000 women who rely on the abortion provider for breast and cervical cancer screenings every
year.[7] Never mind that according to a fact-check the same year
from the *Washington Post*—hardly a publication sympathetic
to the pro-life cause—not one Planned Parenthood facility in
America was certified to perform mammograms.[8]

In any case, pro-life proposals to defund Planned Parenthood have never aimed to eliminate or even cut funding for women's health programs. They only seek to redirect public funding from abortion providers to federally qualified health centers, which don't do abortions but do provide a much more comprehensive array of health services (including mammograms[9]) than Planned Parenthood offers.

The abortion industry's moral panic turned into outright hysteria in 2022, when the Supreme Court voted to overturn *Roe*:

- "Women will die," former Secretary of State Hillary Clinton told *CBS Mornings* cohost Gayle King. "Women will die."
- The medical journal *Lancet* asserted not only that women will die but also "[the ruling's author, Supreme Court Justice Samuel] Alito and his supporters will have women's blood on their hands."[10]
- U.S. senator Jacky Rosen (D-Nev.) said, "Women will die because of this . . . especially women without access to health care, without access to insurance, without access to the means to go travel for an abortion."[11]
- Physician and speaker Dr. Liz Lyster bizarrely asserted, "If more women have babies, more women will die."[12]
- Vox went so far as to call abortion restrictions "structural violence against women," arguing that without access to legal abortion, "more women will die."[13]

One of the strangest reactions came from *USA Today* Voices editor Casey Blake, who wrote:

> Burned at the stake or by a thousand legislative cuts, women will die at the hands of a court that

is so comfortable in [its] power that it won't challenge the wicked spell cast at its conception: the curse of a nation built only for white men, where a belief in women's basic humanity isn't a prerequisite to decide their fate, and a belief in witchcraft and the right kinds of rape can't cancel you, even centuries on.[14]

Huh?

As much as abortion supporters insist that abortion bans and restrictions kill women, the tragic irony is the abortion industry's business actually is killing people—the tiniest and most fragile people, whose hearts are stopped by tools, implements, pills, and poisons. In short, abortion advocates' twisted logic amounts to, "If we aren't allowed to kill people, people will die!"

Abortion proponents don't usually say just *how* women will die without access to abortion. They merely substitute repetition for substance and volume for evidence. When they do attempt to explain how abortion bans kill, they usually argue that:

1. Women facing crisis pregnancies will resort to dangerous, unsafe, back-alley, coat-hanger-induced abortions that threaten their lives.
2. Women who face life-threatening health conditions while pregnant will die without having abortions.

Both claims are demonstrably false. Remember these three points as you explain that abortion bans don't kill people; abortion does.

Point 1: Women Aren't Dying after Having Back-Alley Abortions Because *Roe* Was Overturned

After the Supreme Court released the *Dobbs v. Jackson Women's Health Organization* ruling reversing *Roe*, U.S. representative Alexandria Ocasio-Cortez (AOC) tweeted, "Overturning *Roe* and outlawing abortions will never make them go away. It only makes them more dangerous for the poor + marginalized. People will die because of this decision."[15]

It's a point abortion supporters have argued for decades, not because it's accurate but because it's effective. Most people are uncomfortable with abortion. They don't want to have an abortion. They don't want their wives, girlfriends, daughters, and sisters to have abortions. They prefer not to even think about abortion.

But actually opposing abortion comes with a cost. If you're pro-life, perhaps you can't vote for the political party you've long supported. Maybe you don't want to be labeled a "religious zealot." Certainly, nobody wants to become the latest victim of cancel culture.

So for those who don't like abortion but lack the moral courage to stand up for human life, AOC's argument gives the perfect out. If abortion bans don't prevent abortions anyway, you don't have any moral obligation to support them. Instead, you can present yourself as "sophisticated" for taking a "nuanced" middle-ground approach to a hot-button issue. You can feel free to keep voting for pro-abortion candidates without a troubled conscience. And you can insist that the best way to reduce the number of abortions isn't by banning abortion; it's by enacting some pet legislation, typically involving massive taxpayer funding.

Certainly, any contribution government programs make toward saving lives from abortion is welcomed. But our ultimate goal isn't to reduce the number of abortions; it's to end abortion altogether. One dismembered child is one too many. There is no room for nuance when it comes to violence against children.

Imagine saying, "Look, you're never going to end child abuse and neglect. So instead of criminalizing it, let's pursue common-ground solutions with abusers, reducing their need to beat their kids." It's no less ridiculous to deny legal protections to children simply because they haven't yet passed through the birth canal. There's plenty of evidence showing that abortion prohibitions and restrictions *do* prevent abortions. The number of monthly abortions in Texas dropped by more than 2,700 in the months following the implementation of the Texas Heartbeat Act.[16] Some women almost certainly left the state for abortions, and others might have had illegal abortions. But 6 to 10 months after the law was implemented, the number of live births increased by 5,000 compared with the three-year average.[17]

According to Catholic University of America assistant professor of social research Dr. Michael New:

> A substantial body of academic research shows that legal protections of pre-born children reduce abortion rates. Poland, which has some of the strongest pro-life laws in Europe, also has one of the lowest abortion rates in Europe. Ireland, which was legally protecting pre-born children until 2018, also had low abortion rates. Even in the United States, there is good research showing that a range of state-level incremental pro-life laws including limits on Medicaid funding of abortion, parental involvement laws, and

properly designed informed consent laws all reduce the incidence of abortion.[18]

So abortion restrictions and bans do prevent abortions, but what about AOC's claims that legalizing abortion stops countless preventable deaths of women who desperately resort to illegal, back-alley abortions? Abortion advocates are quick to insist there's nothing pro-life about subjecting thousands of women each year to deaths that could have been prevented by keeping abortion "safe and legal."

During the confirmation hearings for Supreme Court Justice Brett Kavanaugh, U.S. senator Dianne Feinstein (D-Calif.) claimed as many as 1.2 million American women died after undergoing illegal abortions in the 1950s and 1960s—until her spokesperson admitted the senator made a mistake.[19] Both Planned Parenthood and the American College of Obstetricians and Gynecologists (ACOG) have argued that prior to *Roe* legalizing abortion in all 50 U.S. states, thousands of women died from unsafe, illegal abortions every year.[20] The numbers are pure fiction.

A *Washington Post* fact-check analysis sourced Planned Parenthood's bogus claim to nearly 100-year-old data compiled by abortion advocate Frederick Taussig way back in 1936. Taussig's methodology was not exactly rigorous. He first tallied 912 deaths following abortions in 1927–28. Because only 13 states tracked illegal abortion-related deaths in 1927, he extrapolated the findings to the rest of the country to arrive at a total of more than 3,500 deaths. He then rounded the number up to 4,000 and doubled it under the assumption that half of all abortion-related deaths were not reported.[21]

The *Washington Post* gave Planned Parenthood's and the ACOG's botched-abortion body count argument a rating of four "Pinocchios":

[Former Planned Parenthood President Leana] Wen is a doctor, and the ACOG is made up of doctors. They should know better than to peddle statistics based on data that predates the advent of antibiotics. Even given the fuzzy nature of the data and estimates, there is no evidence that in the years immediately preceding the Supreme Court's decision, thousands of women died every year in the United States from illegal abortions. . . . These numbers were debunked in 1969—50 years ago—by a statistician celebrated by Planned Parenthood. There's no reason to use them today.[22]

But there is a big reason to use debunked data: Abortion is a multibillion-dollar industry.

"The widespread belief that tens of thousands of women were dying from illegal abortions was a lie propagated mainly by two individuals . . . Larry Lader and Bernard Nathanson, co-founders of NARAL," said former abortionist and Planned Parenthood medical director Dr. Kathi Aultman. "He admitted, 'When we spoke of [deaths due to illegal abortion], it was always 5,000 to 10,000 per year. I confess I knew the figures were totally false.'"[23] Nathanson continued, "The overriding concern was to get the laws [banning abortion] eliminated, and anything within reason that had to be done was permissible."[24]

Point 2: Abortion Is Never Necessary to Save a Woman's Life

Just weeks after *Roe* was overturned, 18-weeks-pregnant Amanda Zurawski was diagnosed with an "incompetent cervix," meaning there was no hope for saving the life of her baby. The Texas Heartbeat Act prevented Zurawski from having an abortion, and within days, she developed sepsis. Doctors then induced delivery. Her baby died not long after delivery, and Zurawski then sued the state of Texas for putting her life at risk by denying her access to an abortion.[25]

Zurawski's experience is a tragedy—but not one that required the killing of an innocent baby. Pro-life states that prohibit abortion *always* permit emergency medical treatment for a mother, even in the tragic cases where the death of her baby is an unavoidable consequence of the treatment.

"Under the laws of Texas and all other pro-life states, doctors are advised to exercise their reasonable medical judgment to determine [whether] a woman needs to be delivered of her unborn child in order to protect her life," said Charlotte Lozier Institute senior fellow and director of medical affairs Dr. Ingrid Skop, who has practiced obstetrics and gynecology in Texas. "[P]ro-abortion activists continue spreading misinformation, confusing physicians and the general public."[26]

In other words, yes, Zurawski suffered a life-threatening health condition. But no, abortion was not the solution. Directly killing her child was unnecessary. Zurawski was permitted to—and in fact did—undergo an early delivery.

Early induction to save the mother's life is allowed not just by state laws but also by the United States Conference of Catholic Bishops' Ethical and Religious Directives, which are used by Catholic hospitals under fire for their pro-life policies. According to Directive Number 47, "Operations, treatments, and medications that have as their direct purpose the cure of a proportionately serious pathological condition of a pregnant woman are permitted when they cannot be safely postponed until the unborn child is viable, even if they will result in the death of the unborn child."[27]

It's disingenuous to justify a million abortions a year on unusual medical emergencies. But when those rare cases do emerge, an expectant mother facing potentially catastrophic health outcomes can take comfort in knowing that whether it's an ectopic pregnancy, sepsis, uterine cancer, or any other emergency, her doctor can provide the care she needs without deliberately killing her baby.

"It's what we call the principle of double effect," explained Tepeyac Center OB-GYN Dr. Lorna Cvetkovic in an interview with the Catholic News Agency. "You can . . . do the procedure that will save the mother's life. Your intent is not to destroy that pregnancy; your intent is to keep her healthy."[28]

Back in 1980, former U.S. Surgeon General C. Everett Koop said, "In my 36 years of pediatric surgery, I have never known of one instance where the child had to be aborted to save the mother's life."[29] The medical field's ability to save mothers' (and babies') lives without resorting to abortion has only improved since then.

Point 3: The Supreme Court Overturned *Roe* Back in 2022, and Not One Woman Has Died Because She Couldn't Get an Abortion

The assertion that overturning *Roe* would kill thousands of women every year was an effective talking point as long as *Roe* was the law of the land. But the *Dobbs* ruling defanged the argument: Abortion has been illegal in parts of the country for years now, and the abortion industry hasn't identified a single woman killed by abortion bans or restrictions.

If Planned Parenthood could identify even one woman who died because of abortion restrictions, the media would run wall-to-wall coverage and there would be riots in the streets. But pro-lifers can name countless women who have died following legal abortions.[30] The reality is—legal or illegal—there's no such thing as a safe abortion.

The myth has been exposed. So abortion advocates desperate to save the narrative that abortion saves lives have attempted to redefine treatment for miscarriage complications as abortion. "Medical groups note that some women who miscarry their pregnancies need abortion procedures," read an article in the *Baltimore Sun* shortly after *Roe* was overturned.[31]

Of course, there's a big difference between recovering the remains of a baby who has died and actually killing the child. But when reality TV star Jessa Duggar Seewald revealed she suffered what's known as a "missed miscarriage" (meaning she did not naturally deliver her child's body after her baby died), abortion advocates pounced. Due to a history of hemorrhage, Seewald had a D&C procedure to remove her deceased child from her womb and lower the risk of further complications.[32] Media outlets around the world responded by accusing Seewald—a well-known pro-lifer—of having had an abortion. And not just an abortion, but a *lifesaving* abortion:

- "Health care for me but not for thee: a Duggar had an abortion," wrote the *Arkansas Times*.[33]
- "Jessa Duggar Reveals She Had a Life-Saving Abortion in Emotional New Video," read the original headline for a *Parade* article.
- "Jessa Duggar reveals she had to undergo a life-saving abortion after miscarriage," wrote *The Daily Mail*.[34]
- "Jessa Duggar Seewald Had an Abortion, Even If She Won't Say the Word," is how *Jezebel* described the case. "Over the weekend, the evangelical Christian disclosed

her latest pregnancy ended in a D&C, which she and several media outlets framed as a miscarriage. . . . An abortion is how a miscarriage is treated. . . . Abortion is a medical treatment, and when you outlaw it, you threaten people's lives."[35]

Perhaps the most outrageous headline was printed in the *Philadelphia Inquirer*: "In Arkansas, where the Seewalds live, dead fetuses can be aborted, but not living ones."[36]

Academics got in on the act as well.

- New York University law professor Melissa Murray tweeted, "Jessa Duggar discusses her recent miscarriage, which was treated by performing a D&C—that is, an abortion. . . . The Duggars are famously pro-life."[37]
- "The only difference between having a D&C for a spontaneous abortion and an elective abortion is that the intact tissue from the pregnancy may still be there," said Northwestern University medical professor Lauren Streicher.[38]

There's actually another difference—and it's a big one: Elective abortion kills a baby, and a D&C following miscarriage doesn't. "[S]aying that miscarriage care is the same as abortion is like saying that burying a dead child is the same as burying a child alive," wrote *National Review*'s John McCormack. "The process is the same, but the moral acts could not be more different."[39]

Abortion advocates are grasping at straws. They didn't have to make these types of silly arguments when *Roe* was in place. Don't grant them any credibility. The truth is on your side.

What to Say When Abortion Advocates Say Abortion Bans Kill Women:

- Women are not dying after having unsafe back-alley abortions.
- Abortion is never needed to save a woman's life.
- Abortion advocates can't point to a single woman who has died as a result of an abortion ban.

CHAPTER 13

No Hell on Earth

We must love them both, those whose opinions we share
and those whose opinions we reject, for both have labored
in the search for truth, and both have helped us in finding it.

—St. Thomas Aquinas[1]

The fog that often enters your mind as you're walking out of a movie took center stage in Melanie's brain. She and three friends walked out into the dark evening, and her friend, Laura, broke the silence: "Okay, that movie really sucked!" Laughter burst out of the college girls as they walked into the parking lot.

"I can't believe we paid to see that crap!" Melanie exclaimed as she released uncontrollable laughter.

"It was brutal, the lead actor wasn't even cute, and everyone they tried to prop up in the story was a complete loser," said Laura.

"It had no point and I'm dumber for having seen it, but hey, thanks to Laura for suggesting it!" said Melanie.

"Shut up, Melanie," Laura laughed. "Are you going to class tomorrow?"

"I was, but instead I think I'll go to the doctor and ask for antidepressants to get over your stupid movie suggestions," said the feisty Melanie.

"Dang, girl, okay, okay, I'll *never* suggest another movie again, I swear," protested Laura, looking for a way out of her apparently grave sin of movie suggestion.

"You know I still love you, Laura," said Melanie.

"Yeah, I'm totally getting that vibe," said Laura as she and Melanie waved good night to their other two friends.

"No, for real, I'll be in class tomorrow," said Melanie.

"Awesome, love you," said Laura.

"And I really do love you too, Laura," said Melanie with a teasing smile as she waved good night.

As Melanie's head was thrust into her car door, she lost consciousness.

Moments later she came to and was under a large man in the back seat of her own car. He grabbed her ponytail with one hand and was trying to remove her pants with the other. She screamed.

The perpetrator began hitting her and telling her to shut up. She could feel blood pouring out of her head, wounded from when he smashed her into the car door. He started to take her pants off, and she knew what was coming. Melanie was an athlete, was tough, and grew up hunting with her dad and brothers. She occasionally thought about this horrific scenario and what she would do. Now it was happening.

Her hands were pressed down on the sides of her stomach under his weight. He gripped her hair close to her scalp, increasing the pain of her head wound. She loosened her right hand and punched him in the upper gut as she frantically scanned the windows above her, praying someone would see him on top of her.

He lifted up a bit from the punch, and in a panic, Melanie freed her left hand, her strong hand, and grabbed the side of his neck and violently twisted, scratched, and pulled—hope of getting free filled every ounce of her being. He screamed and cussed as he reached for his back pocket, pulled out a .38 revolver, and struck her across the face.

It was just after 4:00 a.m. when Melanie woke up. She prayed this was a nightmare, but her pounding head and bloody face reminded her that life would never be the same from this moment.

She put on her pants and searched for her keys. She had had them in her hand at the start of the attack. Shaking and fighting back tears, she crawled out of the back seat onto the pavement of the parking lot, where she saw her keys underneath the driver's side door. She started her car and drove to her apartment, hurriedly opened her door, and locked it behind her.

She sat on the couch and looked at her phone. No messages or missed calls. As an overwhelming feeling of shame, embarrassment, anger, fear, and loneliness took over her, she broke down in tears. As she sobbed hysterically, she unlocked her phone, dragged her bloody fingers with her rapist's skin under her fingernails across the phone, and tapped 9-1-1.

⁂

Melanie's rapist was captured—committing another rape—within a month. As of the writing of this book, he is still in prison. It was actually the DNA under Melanie's fingernails that helped police identify him. That and his .38 caliber.

Melanie was relieved this monster had been removed from society, but that relief didn't last long. A few weeks later, a pregnancy test came back positive.

Just a sophomore in college, Melanie saw abortion as a responsible option. She had grown up pro-choice. Her parents weren't very political or religious, but she had a good upbringing and was close to her family. She does remember abortion coming up in conversation with her parents and her uncle, a physician. The essence of the dialogue was that abortion wasn't great, but it should be an option. And, of course, it's necessary in cases of rape.

Melanie's parents were loving people, and without them Melanie could not have made it through the initial trauma of the rape. They discussed abortion with her, and everyone agreed it was the best option. Melanie also confided in a professor who confirmed that she should get an abortion.

Melanie visited her OB-GYN for treatment for her injuries and asked where she could get an abortion. Her college town did not have an abortion provider, but fortunately, there was one in a town about 75 miles away. She called and made an appointment.

While Melanie's parents affirmed her decision to have the abortion, she didn't feel right about asking them to drive her. So over a cappuccino, she asked Laura to drive her. Melanie knew Laura's family was Christian and pro-life, but she didn't know what Laura thought about abortion. The subject had never come up in any of their conversations—either in college or during their high school days together.

"Of course I'll drive you, Melanie," said Laura in a low tone, to Melanie's great relief.

On a beautiful Sunday afternoon, two days before the abortion, Laura and Melanie met at a park for a much-needed outing for Melanie, which included a picnic of Chipotle tacos and homemade cookies, something of a tradition for the two of them.

"Has anyone told you not to have an abortion?" Laura asked after they finished eating.

"No, not really," Melanie replied. "Why would they?"

"I don't know. I was just wondering. There's no real reason to do anything else after the hell you've been through."

"Why do you ask?" Melanie pressed. "You're my best friend. If you don't think I should do it, tell me."

"No, it's not that at all. It's just that we're all—me included—telling you to get an abortion. Everybody in your life, really."

"Yeah, probably because it's the only way to move on," answered Melanie.

Laura nodded in agreement as she gazed at a volleyball game being played across the park. "What would happen if you didn't?"

"Well, I'd have my rapist's baby," Melanie answered. "I wouldn't be able to finish school, and I'd be a single mom with no money."

"I'm not saying that," Laura assured her. "I understand abortion is probably the best option, but a question keeps burning inside me."

"What is it?" asked Melanie, followed by a long awkward silence.

"Do women do it?" Laura asked.

"Do what?"

With a look of embarrassment and almost shame, Laura asked, "Do women who have gotten pregnant from rape ever choose life? Does it ever happen?"

"You don't want me to get the abortion. Just say it, Laura!" Melanie said.

"I'm not saying that. If everyone in your life who cares about you is telling you the same thing, it's probably the right thing to do, but in two days none of us can take it back."

"I get it, Laura, and I guess it's good to raise the question. But I can't raise a kid," said Melanie.

"What about adoption?" Laura suggested.

"I would never give my baby up for adoption," Melanie quickly replied.

Laura looked up at her slowly and said, "You know I love you, right?"

"I know you do," answered Melanie, staring at the ground.

"Then which is it?" asked Laura softly.

"What do you mean?"

"You said you'd have to raise your rapist's baby without the abortion but would never give *your* baby up for adoption. Which is it? Is it his baby? Your baby? Both? Or neither because of the horrific way the pregnancy happened?"

The first questioning of conventional wisdom of rape requiring abortion sent Melanie on a journey she didn't expect. With only a few days until her scheduled abortion, she decided to do something exceedingly difficult for most rape victims to do shortly following their trauma. She *thought* about it.

Melanie knew Laura sincerely loved her and had no agenda, and that's what troubled her so much. It wasn't "Melanie's side" vs. "Laura's side." It was actually thinking about both paths before choosing.

She decided to discuss the matter with both her professor and her parents. All of them exploded with fear and a strong insistence that she get the abortion. There was zero room for considering otherwise. Their passionate refusal to entertain any option other than abortion only drove Melanie to question abortion as the default option all the more.

There was just one day left before Melanie's abortion appointment. At a loss from her conversations with her parents and scholastic mentor, Melanie tearfully picked her up phone and typed:

"Do women choose life after rape?"

One of the first articles she clicked on revealed the rape statistics in the United States and broke down how many pregnancies come from rape. Her jaw dropped when she saw that 50 percent of all pregnant rape victims choose life.[2] She read and re-read the stat. *Fifty percent,* she thought.

Her family and her professor responded to the mere possibility of choosing life as though she were an alien. No woman could do this . . .

. . . yet half of them do.

Melanie read about kids and adults conceived in rape. She read stories from women who were raped and chose life. And women who were raped and chose abortion. She read about adoption. She scrolled the internet for hours. By the time she finished, it became clear. She couldn't go through with it.

Melanie's parents protested, and her professor told her she would never graduate from college. As devastating as this was, Melanie realized her toughness was not stolen in her car that horrific night. The perpetrator could never steal that strength unless she allowed him to. For the first time since the rape, she revisited a part of her that she refused to surrender: *her will to fight.*

She had fought her rapist. She scratched, hit, screamed, and clawed to protect herself. The man—who doesn't deserve to be called a man—had forfeited his rights over the baby. But this baby had a fighter for a mother.

The question now burned inside Melanie: *I fought for myself. Will I fight for my little boy or little girl?*

The following November, Melanie gave birth to a six-pound, seven-ounce baby girl. Two and half years later, seated in the front row of a large auditorium, Melanie turned to her mom to hand over her toddler, who now had braided pigtails.

As Melanie walked onto the stage, she was announced as the valedictorian of her graduating college class. And at the end of her speech, she dedicated the great honor to her daughter. A daughter who represented hope in the midst of hell. A daughter who meant the world to her. A daughter whom she could not imagine living without. A daughter she would always fight for. A daughter she decided to name Laura.

⁂

As we wrote about in the first *What to Say When*, rape is often the first point an abortion supporter brings up, and I (Shawn) believe it comes from a place of compassion.

Rape is the hardest and most emotional part of the abortion debate.

In almost any abortion conversation—at work, around a dinner table, or in a political discussion—rape quickly takes center stage. Abortion advocates use rape to justify *all* abortions. And they've been very successful convincing politicians, women, pastors, and even people who identify as pro-life to support abortion in the case of rape.

We have found there's no topic pro-lifers fear more than rape. Although they are against aborting babies conceived in any situation, they feel ill equipped and uncomfortable defending the pro-life position when abortion supporters present them with "hard cases" (which almost always involve a teenage girl being raped by a violent criminal needing legal abortion as an option).

Abortion supporters turn to the rape argument because it puts them in a seemingly perfect position. They portray abortion opponents as siding with rapists against innocent women. Nearly every government in the world has a rape exception because the government never wants to be on the side of a violent criminal.

Rape cases make up about 1 percent of all abortions each year.[3] However, it is a mistake to dismiss abortions that follow rape simply because they are relatively rare. If you or a loved one are the victim of sexual assault, that "rare" case means everything to you. A key part of recognizing and defending the dignity of rape victims is protecting them from further violence in the form of abortion.

Remember the following truths when rape comes up in an abortion conversation:

Point 1: Rape Is a Terrible Crime, and the Rapist Is a Criminal

Sometimes pro-life people skip over the crime and harsh reality of rape to start arguing for the humanity of the baby. But remember, the woman is a living victim. We need to acknowledge that early in the conversation, both in our tone and in our words.

Affirm that the man is the guilty party and should be in the penitentiary. He is the criminal, and the victim is innocent. *She did nothing wrong.* It is critical to say this because sometimes the person defending abortion in cases of rape is a victim of rape herself, and victims sometimes blame themselves.

Clearly pointing out that the guilty party is the rapist, who deserves to go to prison, affirms the atrocity of rape and is a crucial part of the pro-life answer.

Point 2: Abortion Supporters Believe a Heartfelt Myth That Abortion Removes Rape

Abortion supporters genuinely believe abortion will help rape victims move on with their lives. They see abortion as necessary to give an ounce of consolation after the evil crime that left the victim pregnant against her will. They might view you as disconnected or heartless for not understanding this harsh reality.

Point 3: When It Comes to Rape, Abortion Supporters Will Understandably Argue with Passion and Emotion

When rape and abortion come up, know that abortion supporters will argue passionately and emotionally (most likely as soon as you say that you don't support abortion even in cases of rape). When dramatic statements and accusations about your intentions are made, endure them in loving silence, be kind, and steer the conversation toward the real people involved in the tragedy of rape—the rapist, the victim, and the baby. We need stronger laws (and enforcement of laws) to protect women and punish rapists—not more abortion.

The Rapist

Rapists deserve to go to the penitentiary. Or maybe to meet Sonny from *The Godfather*, who smashed his brother-in-law's head with a trash can lid after he found out the brother-in-law was beating his sister. Obviously, we're not encouraging that, but the scene accurately shows how most people feel about men who abuse women. The point is, no one is on the side of the rapist. Casually skipping over the crime he committed is irresponsible when defending the unborn.

What to Say: *The rapist should go to prison.*

The Victim

The woman is the victim and our primary focus when discussing rape and abortion. Abortion advocates assume we couldn't care less about the victims of rape and only care about unborn children. The exact opposite is true. We love rape victims so much we want to give them real options, so they don't fall into the temptation to try to correct evil with more evil.

What to Say: *The abortion will not remove the pain of the rape.*

The Baby

When a woman becomes pregnant after rape, we need to remind abortion supporters that a baby exists. If the baby didn't exist, abortion would not be an option. Without a baby, there can be no abortion. The question remains, "What do we do with a baby conceived in rape?"

The baby is not responsible and should not be punished for the circumstances of her conception. No child would choose to be conceived in rape.

We do not gradually gain dignity or value during gestation. We're not mutual funds or stocks that get more valuable over time. We come into existence at conception and then grow.

Likewise, our dignity is not based on the circumstances of our conception. If your parents are healthy, Harvard-educated homeowners who conceived you on their honeymoon in Paris, you are not more valuable than someone conceived in an apartment by two people struggling to make ends meet. You're not more valuable than a child conceived in rape.

Scientifically, there is no difference between you and a child conceived in rape. We are all equal in dignity—no matter the circumstances of our conception. Except for rape, we typically have *more* respect for kids who were not conceived in the best of situations but who overcome great odds in life. Except for rape, we seek to protect kids with troubled or abusive backgrounds even more. Except for rape, we never diminish a child's dignity because of the crimes of her father. We certainly would not say she *never should have been born* because of who her father is.

When else do we punish a child for the sins of his or her father? When do we hold a baby accountable for the behavior of his dad? If an amusement park attendant stopped a pregnant woman from getting on a roller coaster, and she calmly said, "It's okay. My daughter was conceived in rape," would the attendant let her on the ride? Would the bartender serve her ten whiskeys? Would the skydiving company make an exception and let her jump? No.

We treat human beings with more dignity than we sometimes get credit for, but all of that seems to go out the window when someone is discussing rape and abortion. It is supposed to be a no-brainer for why abortion is not just needed but good. In other scenarios, we would not look down on someone as a human being if we found out her father was a criminal.

Rape and abortion punish a unique, innocent human being like no other scenario in our culture.

A baby conceived in rape will always live life as a result of that rape. He or she will go to school, play sports, fail, love, struggle, and reach highs and lows no one can or ought to predict when the child is first conceived. The road for a baby conceived in rape is a difficult one, but it is hers alone. No criminal, the biological father included, can be used to justify denying her the right to life.

What to Say When abortion supporters bring up rape: *Our human dignity is not determined by the circumstances of our conception. No child should be devalued because of the sins of the father.*

❧

Arguments against abortion in cases of rape make sense. But real human experience is powerful too.

Hundreds of students—half pro-life and half pro-choice—poured into a packed college lecture hall to hear two women who had been raped speak. One had an abortion, and one gave her baby up for adoption. Each shared the horrific experience of rape. Each shared the experience of considering abortion. And each explained the reason for her decision.

Both used logic without much emotion in sharing why they decided to have or not to have an abortion. Most students, even the pro-life students, understood why the rape victim who chose abortion did so. There was a spirit of compassion, not judgment, in the room.

The forum seemed to be wrapping up until the woman who chose abortion said, "Now many people encouraged me and supported me in my decision. They understood, and most women told me they would do the same if they were in my position. This is, after all, why we have legal abortion. But no one, including myself, ever considered what would happen after my abortion. No one ever considered that I would be adding an anniversary to my life."

The students homed in on the term *anniversary*.

We have worked with many victims of rape, and all of them remember the date of their rape. They all have an annual anniversary, a reminder of the horrible event. Similarly, we have met thousands of postabortive women, and almost all of them know the anniversary of their abortion.

The woman who was raped and chose abortion explained that she did not want her baby to remind her of her tragic rape. She wanted the rape in her past.

She passionately explained how the opposite happened. The rape and the abortion became two parallel traumas that feed off one another. She said that her rape anniversary reminded her of her abortion, and her abortion anniversary reminded her of the rape. She was fighting a double battle because of a decision that was supposed to help her move on from this horrific event but instead magnified her pain. Her testimony ended as she described encountering God and receiving the strength and grace to find hope and healing.

Then the rape victim who chose life and gave her baby up for adoption spoke. She shared the joy of getting updates on her son from his adoptive parents. She shared how close she came to choosing abortion before deciding she couldn't do it. And she described how every event of her son's life is a testament that the rape does not define her. She said her rape anniversary reminds her there is always hope after our worst experiences in life.

The students sat in silence and listened to these two women share the reality of the consequences of rape and abortion. There is no sugarcoating the atrocity of rape or abortion. But an atrocity does not have the ultimate power to change our nature—that we are hardwired to protect our children. Their courage to share their real-life experience is too often absent from the discussion on rape and abortion. No one thinks about the two anniversaries feeding—positively or negatively—off one another.

These two women's experiences illuminate the victims in this story and demonstrate why abortion can never comfort, console, or solve a woman's problem.

Now let's look at the experience of the child.

❧

The Planned Parenthood staff gathered outside to hear the speakers at a pro-life event on the sidewalk in front of their workplace the day of the *Roe v. Wade* Supreme Court anniversary.

The last speaker was a young woman in her early 20s. She shared how she was conceived by the act of a criminal when her mother was raped at age 14. Her father was incarcerated. After nearly deciding to have an abortion, the teenage mom instead gave her daughter up for adoption. More than two decades later, the young woman who nearly lost her life to abortion conveyed the immense gratitude she had for her mom choosing adoption and expressed her love for her adoptive parents.

"Something in my life never changed since the day my mom was raped," the young woman said. "From that day on, I am a result of rape. I cannot change that. I was conceived in rape and will be forever a product of rape."

She then turned to the Planned Parenthood workers standing in the parking lot listening attentively. "Do you see me? Do you look at me differently since I told you how I was conceived? I stand here before you still a result of rape, just as I was in the womb. Do you believe my life is worth living because every day I live I do so because of rape? But that rape does not define my dignity or the dignity of any other child who is conceived in rape."

As with the women who were victims of rape, silence poured over both the pro-life audience and the Planned Parenthood workers looking on. The young woman's powerful testimony spoke the truth that our culture has forgotten. She went on to get married and have children of her own, ensuring the impact of her mother's courageous decision to choose life was generational.

৯৳

Once we know how to effectively discuss rape and abortion, all other pro-abortion arguments become easy to counter. We've made these points with thousands of people in diversified scenarios, including abortion workers on the sidewalk, college campuses, and even a pro-abortion NBC News reporter who said off the record she had never heard a pro-life case against abortion in cases of rape that she agreed with until now.

Trust that when we share the truth with love, minds can be illuminated and hearts can be changed.

What to Say When Rape and Abortion Come Up:

- The rapist should go to prison.
- Human dignity is not defined by the circumstances of our conception.
- In no other scenario do we punish a baby for the crimes of his or her father.
- Abortion does not remove rape; it adds to the pain.

৯৳

On the June day when *Roe vs. Wade* was overturned, I got up from my beach chair in Galveston, ran through the rattlesnake pit, and set up my equipment for a day of media interviews.

The first interview was a major media source that interviewed me and a woman who led a global organization who was devastated at the overturning of *Roe*. She was very gracious and respectful of me, and I felt the interview went quite well and was shocked that she never brought up rape. She was the only abortion advocate I had ever been across from in an interview who didn't bring up rape, and it was the day *Roe* was overturned.

As we were wrapping up and saying our good-byes to the reporter, my opponent said, "Wait! I have one more point I forgot!" *Here we go*, I thought to myself.

The reporter said she would allow it, and we began recording. The woman's demeanor changed grimly, and she looked into the camera and said with a different tone, "I'm tired of people like Mr. Carney forcing 14-year-old rape victims to have babies."

For the first time in my life in an interview, I felt a surge of something I've never felt as I'm speaking to an abortion advocate: *anger*. Her comment angered me but not because she was insulting me. I'm plenty used to folks telling me I don't care about 14-year-old rape victims. That happens all the time. Instead, it was another point of frustration that I had never realized and wish I had put in the first *What to Say When*.

Inwardly, I was boiling, but outwardly I was calm—part of being both Irish and Southern; we know how to save face. I asked the reporter if I could respond, and she agreed. I looked at the camera and asked, "Have you ever looked into the eyes of a 14-year-old rape victim?"

It was silent.

"No."

"Does your organization offer any help or assistance or referrals for rape victims?" I continued.

"No," again.

I looked into the camera and said, "Rape is serious. We work with rape victims of all ages. I'm tired of detached abortion advocates sensationalizing rape and exploiting rape victims, whom they have no contact with, so they can sell abortions."

The reporter ended the interview.

Her accusation of not caring about a woman who is raped, after being accused of that thousands of times in my life, recalled the countless rape victims who have been helped by 40 Days for Life and the pro-life movement at large. We are the first ones to encounter them when they go in for an abortion, the first ones to help them if they want to choose life, and the first ones to offer hope and healing if they go through with the abortion. We're there for them and always will be.

When defending the beautiful reality of human life, it's especially important for you and me not to have an ivory-tower connection with the abortion crisis. It's easy to fall into with more than 70 million abortions in the world every year. But this cause is personal and individual. Rape is devastating, abortion is devastating, and discussing them must first come from the heart.

Intellectually, the pro-life message is simple and easy. But the success of it is dependent on the love in our hearts, no matter what the circumstances are.

There is no greater inspiration than a mother who fights for her child. If Melanie can go through the trauma of rape and still have the faith and fortitude to fight for her child, how could we cower at any opportunity to be a voice for those who have no voice but ours?

If this really is about life and death, how could we *not* do something? How could we *not* say something? How could we *not* have the courage to question—as Laura did—the notion that abortion is the answer to our problems?

The fight for the unborn is not a battle of arguments or logic. If that were the case, we'd have won decades ago. It is a battle of will. Our wills direct our souls—for good or for evil.

If we entrust our wills to God, His goodness, His love, and His mercy, He will show us that there is no hell on earth that His light cannot overcome.

That light is what saved baby Laura, and that light is what will end abortion in our cities, states, nations, and world.

Acknowledgments

Thank you to the 40 Days for Life board of directors for their enthusiasm and support to get this book out during such a busy time for our mission and a historic time for the pro-life movement. Special thanks to our legal team led by General Counsel Matt Britton.

What would we do without our wonderful copyeditor Lisa Parnell? You are gold! Every time we work with you, we hope we have another book in us! And we are grateful to Jeanette Gillespie for designing the book cover.

Thank you to the entire 40 Days for Life team who make this work possible and the local campaign leaders who are our inspiration to do this work every day.

Finally, to our wonderful wives. Writing any book, but especially one like this, is time consuming and takes much sacrifice on top of our other work responsibilities. Thank you for your support, feedback, and love. You always know what to say to keep us going.

Endnotes

Epigraph
1. Bruce Catton, *The Civil War* (New York: Mariner Books, 2004), 4.

Introduction
1. https://www.azquotes.com/quote/124726.
2. The Guttmacher Institute, "Unintended Pregnancy and Abortion Worldwide," March 2022, https://www.guttmacher.org/fact-sheet/induced-abortion-worldwide.

Chapter 1
1. Fr. Richard Heilman, "70 Saints' Quotes to Elevate Your Game!," Roman Catholic Man, October 4, 2015, https://romancatholicman.com/wp/70-saints-quotes-to-elevate-your-game/.
2. Oriana González, "Anti-abortion pregnancy centers are expanding in the post-*Roe* era," *Axios*, August 19, 2022, https://www.axios.com/2022/08/19/crisis-pregnancy-centers-abortion-roe-health-care.
3. University of California San Francisco, Abortion Facility Database, https://www.ansirh.org/abortion-facility-database.
4. González, "Anti-abortion pregnancy centers are expanding in the post-*Roe* era."
5. https://www.nytimes.com/2022/06/25/us/trigger-laws-abortion-states-roe.html.
6. Rick Rojas and Alan Blinder, "Alabama Abortion Ban Is Temporarily Blocked by a Federal Judge," October 29, 2019, *The New York Times*, https://www.nytimes.com/2019/10/29/us/alabama-abortion-ban.html.

7. Danica Jefferies, JoElla Carman, and Nigel Chiwaya, "Abortion law tracker: See where the procedure is currently legal, banned or restricted in the U.S.," *NBC News*, June 30, 2022, https://www.nbcnews.com/data-graphics/abortion-state-tracking-trigger-laws-bans-restrictions-rcna36199.

8. Planned Parenthood Action, "Preparing for Your Abortion Access House Party," https://www.plannedparenthoodaction.org/rightfully-ours/bans-off-our-bodies/house-party-toolkit/prepare-abortion-access-house-party.

9. 40 Days for Life, "Post-*Roe* America," https://www.40daysforlife.com/en/postroeamerica.

10. Caitlin O'Kane, "New York passes law allowing abortions at any time if mother's health is at risk," *CBS News*, updated on January 24, 2019, https://www.cbsnews.com/news/new-york-passes-abortion-bill-late-term-if-mothers-health-is-at-risk-today-2019-01-23/.

11. Nicole Dube, "States Allowing Non-Physicians to Provide Abortion Services," Office of Legislative Research, July 29, 2022, https://www.cga.ct.gov/2022/rpt/pdf/2022-R-0167.pdf.

12. Charlotte Lozier Institute, "Questions and Answers on Born-Alive Abortion Survivors," published April 12, 2021, updated January 27, 2023, https://lozierinstitute.org/questions-and-answers-on-born-alive-abortion-survivors/.

Chapter 2

1. Samuel Alito, *Dobbs v. Jackson Women's Health Organization*, Supreme Court of the United States, June 24, 2022, https://www.supremecourt.gov/opinions/21pdf/19-1392_6j37.pdf.

2. Kyle Morris, Sam Dorman, "Over 63 million abortions have occurred in the US since Roe v. Wade decision in 1973," *Fox News*, May 4, 2022, https://www.foxnews.com/politics/abortions-since-roe-v-wade.

3. Charlotte Lozier Institute, "Questions and Answers on Born-Alive Abortion Survivors," published April 12, 2021, updated January 27, 2023, https://lozierinstitute.org/questions-and-answers-on-born-alive-abortion-survivors/.

4. "Testimony of the Human Trafficking Prevention Project," University of Baltimore, February 22, 2022, https://mgaleg.maryland.gov/cmte_testimony/2022/hgo/1fT7Hn_bjT8TUbDhlXtP35SlbxFSjF-Yj.pdf found via https://www.frc.org/get.cfm?i=PV20A05.

5. Josh Gerstein and Alexander Ward, "Supreme Court has voted to overturn abortion rights, draft opinion shows," *Politico*, published May 2, 2022, updated May 3, 2022, https://www.politico.com/news/2022/05/02/supreme-court-abortion-draft-opinion-00029473.

6. Kevin D. Williamson, "Yes, Overturn Roe," *National Review*, May 17, 2021, https://www.nationalreview.com/corner/yes-overturn-roe/ found via https://www.christianunion.org/the-magazine/3288-as-law,-roe-was-a -bad-ruling-that-always-had-to-go.

7. David G. Savage, "Where Roe went wrong: A sweeping new abortion right built on a shaky legal foundation," May 3, 2022, https://www.latimes.com/politics/story/2022-05-03/how-roe-vs -wade-went-wrong-broad-new-right-to-abortion-rested-on-a-shaky -legal-foundation found via https://www.christianunion.org/the-maga zine/3288-as-law,-roe-was-a-bad-ruling-that-always-had-to-go.

8. Harry Blackmun, *Roe v. Wade*, Supreme Court of the United States, January 22, 1973, https://supreme.justia.com/cases/federal/us/4 10/113/.

9. Ibid.

10. Alito, *Dobbs v. Jackson Women's Health Organization*.

11. Harry Blackmun, *Roe v. Wade*, Supreme Court of the United States, January 22, 1973, https://supreme.justia.com/cases/federal/us/4 10/113/.

12. Deepa Shivaram, "Roe established abortion rights. 20 years later, Casey paved the way for restrictions," *NPR*, May 6, 2022, https://www .npr.org/2022/05/06/1096885897/roe-established-abortion-rights-20 -years-later-casey-paved-the-way-for-restricti.

13. Blackmun, *Roe v. Wade*.

14. Hannah Echols, "UAB Hospital delivers record-breaking premature baby," University of Alabama at Birmingham, November 10, 2021, https://www.uab.edu/news/health/item/12427-uab-hospital -delivers-record-breaking-premature-baby.

15. EWTN Pro-Life Weekly, "Mississippi Attorney General Lynn Fitch on Supreme Court Abortion Case," September 25, 2021, https:// www.youtube.com/watch?v=fw3mONWPPqE.

16. Lewis Powell, "Akron v. Akron Ctr. for Reprod. Health," Supreme Court of the United States, June 15, 1983, https://supreme .justia.com/cases/federal/us/462/416/.

17. Rich Lowry, "Why Roe v. Wade is a travesty of constitutional law," *New York Post*, July 6, 2018, https://nypost.com/2018/07/06/why-roe-v-wade-is-a-travesty-of-constitutional-law/.

18. Houston Christian University, "The End of a Nightmare. The U.S. Supreme Court Overturns Roe v. Wade," December 16, 2022, https://hc.edu/news-and-events/2022/12/16/the-end-of-a-nightmare-the-u-s-supreme-court-overturns-roe-v-wade/.

19. Ruth Rubio-Marín, "'Notorious RBG': A conversation with United States Supreme Court Justice Ruth Bader Ginsburg," International Journal of Constitutional Law, October 30, 2017, https://academic.oup.com/icon/article/15/3/602/4582632.

20. Samuel Alito, *Dobbs v. Jackson Women's Health Organization*, Supreme Court of the United States, June 24, 2022, https://www.supremecourt.gov/opinions/21pdf/19-1392_6j37.pdf.

21. Ibid.

22. SuperTalk Missouri, "AG Lynn Fitch - Roe V Wade," June 27, 2022, https://www.youtube.com/watch?v=7Nh646xy3nM.

23. Alito, *Dobbs v. Jackson Women's Health Organization*.

24. Ibid.

25. Cardinal Joseph Mindszenty, "Mother," *EWTN*, https://www.ewtn.com/catholicism/library/mother-11253.

26. https://www.youtube.com/watch?v=fw3mONWPPqE.

27. Ibid.

28. Choose Life, https://www.chooselifems.org/pregnancy-centers/ https://www.chooselifems.org/pregnancy-centers/.

Chapter 3

1. Dr. Bernard Nathanson, "An ex-abortionist speaks," *Catholic News Agency*, https://www.catholicnewsagency.com/resource/55401/an-ex-abortionist-speaks.

2. Jordan E. Pratt, "Court Grants Certiorari in Mississippi Abortion Case, Dismisses Title X Cases," the Federalist Society, May 18, 2021, https://fedsoc.org/commentary/fedsoc-blog/court-grants-certiorari-in-mississippi-abortion-case-dismisses-title-x-cases.

3. Josh Gerstein and Alexander Ward, "Supreme Court has voted to overturn abortion rights, draft opinion shows," *Politico*, published May 2, 2022, updated May 3, 2022, https://www.politico.com/news/2022/05/02/supreme-court-abortion-draft-opinion-00029473.

4. Planned Parenthood, May 13, 2022, https://twitter.com/PPFA /status/1525113800508289024.

5. Planned Parenthood, May 28, 2022, https://twitter.com/PPFA /status/1530594753712009217; June 11, 2022, https://twitter.com/PP FA/status/1535653122928001025; June 22, 2022, https://twitter.com /PPFA/status/1539640812329267200; June 19, 2022, https://twitter .com/PPFA/status/1538537140702924803; June 12, 2022, https:// twitter.com/PPFA/status/1536108274097000454; June 19, 2022, https: //twitter.com/PPFA/status/1538612585381117953.

6. Kyle Stockard, "It's Time to Destigmatize STIs," 2022, https:// www.liberator.com/blog/destigmatize-stis.html.

7. Planned Parenthood, June 24, 2022, https://web.archive.org /web/20220625020240/https://twitter.com/PPFA.

8. Sarah McCammon, "After Years In the Trenches, Planned Parenthood's Cecile Richards Will Step Down," *NPR*, January 26, 2018, https://www.npr.org/sections/thetwo-way/2018/01/26/580733009 /after-years-in-the-trenches-planned-parenthoods-cecile-richards-will -step-down.

9. Tessa Stuart, "She Made Planned Parenthood a Juggernaut. Now Her Progress Is Being Erased," *Rolling Stone*, July 2, 2022, https://www.rollingstone.com/politics/politics-features/cecile-richards -planned-parenthood-roe-wade-supreme-court-1377046/.

10. Kate Zernike, "Planned Parenthood Names Leana Wen, a Doctor, Its New President," *The New York Times*, September 12, 2018, https://www.nytimes.com/2018/09/12/us/politics/planned-parent hood-president-wen.html.

11. Ibid.

12. Anna Medaris, "Planned Parenthood's former president said the organization wanted to use her miscarriage to cover up the real reason for her departure," *Business Insider*, July 27, 2021, https://www. businessinsider.com/dr-leana-wen-book-planned-parenthood-wanted- use-miscarriage-cover-2021-7.

13. Vanessa Romo, "Planned Parenthood Removes Leana Wen As President After Less Than A Year," *NPR*, July 16, 2019, https:// www.npr.org/2019/07/16/742390932/planned-parenthood-removes -leana-wen-as-president-after-less-than-a-year.

14. Colin Campbell, "Former Baltimore health commissioner Leana Wen, Planned Parenthood resolve dispute over severance, benefits," *Baltimore Sun*, September 18, 2019, https://www.baltimoresun.

com/2019/09/18/former-baltimore-health-commissioner-leana-wen-planned-parenthood-resolve-dispute-over-severance-benefits/.

15. Romo, "Planned Parenthood Removes Leana Wen As President After Less Than A Year."

16. Planned Parenthood, "Alexis McGill Johnson Named Permanent President and CEO of the Planned Parenthood Federation of America and the Planned Parenthood Action Fund," June 26, 2020, https://www.plannedparenthood.org/about-us/newsroom/press-releases/alexis-mcgill-johnson-named-permanent-president-and-ceo-of-the-planned-parenthood-federation-of-america-and-the-planned-parenthood-action-fund.

17. Planned Parenthood, "Alexis McGill Johnson," https://www.plannedparenthood.org/about-us/our-leadership/alexis-mcgill-johnson

18. Alexis McGill Johnson, July 1, 2020, https://twitter.com/alexismcgill/status/1278326263195873280.

19. Alexis McGill Johnson, January 23, 2024, https://twitter.com/alexismcgill/status/1749969851852980373.

20. MSNBC, "Planned Parenthood unveils its first-ever call for SCOTUS reform," May 14, 2023, https://www.youtube.com/watch?v=p_hztE6Rnm8.

21. Al Sharpton, January 22, 2024, https://twitter.com/TheRevAl/status/1749298528919097762.

22. Internet search, Quitter Stories | abortionworker.com.

23. Amy Littlefield, "Where the Pro-Choice Movement Went Wrong," *The New York Times*, December 1, 2021, https://www.nytimes.com/2021/12/01/opinion/abortion-planned-parenthood-naral-roe-v-wade.html found via https://www.teenvogue.com/story/how-abortion-rights-movement-failed.

24. Marian Jones, "The Mainstream Abortion Rights Movement Failed to Prevent the End of Roe," *Teen Vogue*, May 6, 2022, https://www.teenvogue.com/story/how-abortion-rights-movement-failed.

25. Eyal Press, "The Problem with Planned Parenthood," the *New Yorker*, May 8, 2023, https://www.newyorker.com/magazine/2023/05/15/the-problem-with-planned-parenthood.

26. Mary Kekatos, "Woman says she was forced to travel for an abortion despite her fetus's fatal condition," ABC News, June 15, 2023, https://abcnews.go.com/Health/woman-forced-travel-abortion-despite-fetuss-fatal-condition/story?id=100065877.

27. Ibid.

28. Ibid.

29. Ibid.

30. Ibid.

31. Kimya Forouzan, Amy Friedrich-Karnik, Isaac Maddow-Zimet, "The High Toll of US Abortion Bans: Nearly One in Five Patients Now Traveling Out of State for Abortion Care," the Guttmacher Institute, December 2023, https://www.guttmacher.org/2023/12/high-toll-us-abortion-bans-nearly-one-five-patients-now-traveling-out-state-abortion-care.

32. Sarah McCammon, "Even before the Dobbs ruling, more Americans were traveling for abortions," *NPR*, July 21, 2022, https://www.npr.org/2022/07/21/1112609958/even-before-the-dobbs-ruling-more-americans-were-traveling-for-abortions.

33. Eleanor Klibanoff, "Hispanic and teen fertility rates increase after abortion restrictions," *Texas Tribune*, January 26, 2024, https://www.texastribune.org/2024/01/26/texas-abortion-fertility-rate-increase/.

34. Susan Scutti, "Some US women travel hundreds of miles for abortions, analysis finds," CNN, October 4, 2017, https://www.cnn.com/2017/10/03/health/abortion-access-disparities-study/index.html.

35. Emma Goldbert, "These Companies Will Cover Travel Expenses for Employee Abortions," *The New York Times*, August 19, 2022, https://www.nytimes.com/article/abortion-companies-travel-expenses.html.

36. Ibid.

37. Alito, *Dobbs v. Jackson Women's Health Organization*.

38. *At Liberty Podcast*, "How Dismantling Roe Puts Interracial Marriage at Risk," ACLU, June 9, 2022, https://www.aclu.org/podcast/how-dismantling-roe-puts-interracial-marriage-at-risk.

39. Alexandra Martinez, "Birth control, gay and interracial marriage, and more may be at risk if Roe v. Wade falls," *Prism*, May 5, 2022, https://prismreports.org/2022/05/05/civil-rights-roe-v-wade/.

40. Madison Hall and Yoonji Han, "As the Supreme Court overturns Roe v. Wade, some experts fear interracial marriage may be the next target," *Business Insider*, June 24, 2022, https://www.businessinsider.com/roe-wade-loving-virginia-interracial-marriage-scotus-overturns-2022-6.

41. Emma Kinery, "Biden signs bill to protect same-sex and interracial marriages," CNBC, December 13, 2022, https://www.cnbc.com/2022/12/13/biden-signs-respect-for-marriage-act-to-protect-same-sex-interracial-marriages.html.

42. Max Matza, "Respect for Marriage Act: Why interracial marriage is also in the law," BBC News, December 13, 2022, https://www.bbc.com/news/world-us-canada-63801108.

43. Lawrence Hamilton, "Conspiracy vs. Science: A Survey of U.S. Public Beliefs," University of New Hampshire, April 25, 2022, https://carsey.unh.edu/publication/conspiracy-vs-science-a-survey-of-us-public-beliefs

44. 13th Amendment to the U.S. Constitution, January 31, 1865, https://www.archives.gov/milestone-documents/13th-amendment.

45. Michele Goodwin, "No, Justice Alito, Reproductive Justice Is in the Constitution," *The New York Times*, June 26, 2022, https://www.nytimes.com/2022/06/26/opinion/justice-alito-reproductive-justice-constitution-abortion.html.

46. Judge Colleen Kollar-Kotelly, *United States of America v. Lauren Handy*, United States District Court for the District of Columbia, February 6, 2023, https://ecf.dcd.uscourts.gov/cgi-bin/show_public_doc?2022cr0096-167 found via https://www.vox.com/policy-and-politics/2023/2/7/23589355/supreme-court-abortion-dobbs-jackson-handy-united-states-judge-kollar-kotelly.

47. Katha Pollitt, "6 Myths About Abortion," *Time*, November 13, 2014, https://time.com/3582434/6-abortion-myths/.

48. Charlie Nash, "Journalist Says She Would Vote Biden Even 'If He Boiled Babies and Ate Them,'" Mediaite, May 21, 2020, https://www.mediaite.com/politics/journalist-says-she-would-vote-biden-even-if-he-boiled-babies-and-ate-them-taking-back-white-house-is-that-important/.

49. Tim Ahrens, "I am in an ad supporting Issue 1. Cruelty of 'Christians' opposing it is staggering," *The Columbus Dispatch*, published October 31, 2023, updated November 1, 2023, https://www.dispatch.com/story/opinion/columns/guest/2023/10/31/issue-1-rev-tim-ahrens-backlash-resolve-abortion-ad-ohio-hate/71385003007/.

50. Italics in original, ibid.

51. Jack Jenkins, "Planned Parenthood announces new clergy advocacy board members, many from red states," *Religion News Service*, April 13, 2021, https://religionnews.com/2021/04/13/planned-parenthood-announces-new-clergy-advisory-board-members-many-from-red-states/.

52. Latishia James-Portis, https://medium.com/@PurposefullyLJ/about.

53. Jenkins, "Planned Parenthood announces new clergy advocacy board members, many from red states."

54. Rebecca Todd Peters, "Why Falling U.S. Birthrates Are A Good Thing," *Patheos*, May 26, 2018, https://www.patheos.com/blogs/todojustice/2018/05/26/why-falling-u-s-birthrates-are-a-good-thing/.

55. Elle Dowd, https://web.archive.org/web/20240328194303/https://dowdsermonizing.wordpress.com/.

56. Ryan Foley, "Pastor running for Senate: Abortion rights are 'consistent' with my beliefs as a minister," *The Christian Post*, Wednesday, August 26, 2020, https://www.christianpost.com/news/pastor-running-for-senate-abortion-rights-are-consistent-with-my-beliefs-as-a-minister.html.

57. Austin Denean, "Religious divide on abortion debate draws criticism for Biden," *ABC 15 News*, Wednesday, May 4, 2022, https://wpde.com/news/nation-world/religious-divide-on-abortion-debate-draws-criticism-for-president-joe-biden-roe-v-wade-supreme-court-decision-opinion-leak-reproductive-health.

58. Timothy P. Carney, "Biden selection pleases delegates, legalized abortion activists," *Catholic News Agency*, August 25, 2008, https://www.catholicnewsagency.com/news/13630/biden-selection-pleases-delegates-legalized-abortion-activists.

59. Shawna Mizelle, "Biden campaign tries to put abortion in the forefront. But pro-Palestinian protesters interrupted," *CBS News*, January 24, 2024, https://www.cbsnews.com/news/biden-abortion-virginia-pro-palestinian-protesters/.

60. The Satanic Temple, "Satanic Abortion Ritual," https://cdn.shopify.com/s/files/1/0428/0465/files/Abortion_Ritual_Procedure_061322.pdf?v=1657724339.

61. Kelly McClure, "'The Samuel Alito's Mom's Satanic Abortion Clinic' is a thing that exists now," *Salon*, February 15, 2023, https://www.salon.com/2023/02/15/the-samuel-alitos-moms-satanic-abortion-clinic-is-a-thing-that-exists-now/.

62. The Satanic Temple, "TST Health's Name Our Abortion Clinic Fundraiser," https://thesatanictemple.com/pages/new-fundraiser.

63. Bettina di Fiore, "California 'church' founded for sole purpose of worshipping abortion," Live Action, April 18, 2023, https://www.liveaction.org/news/california-church-worshipping-abortion.

64. Kate Scanlon, "Kansas Enacts 'Born-Alive' Bill After Legislature Overrides Governor's Veto," *OSV News*, April 29, 2023, https://www

.osvnews.com/2023/04/29/kansas-enacts-born-alive-bill-after-legislature
-overrides-governors-veto/.

65. Jason Alatidd, "Gov. Laura Kelly vetoes first abortion bill since Kansas voters rejected Value Them Both," *Topeka Capital-Journal*, April 14, 2023, https://www.cjonline.com/story/news/politics /government/2023/04/14/laura-kelly-vetoes-born-alive-abortion-bill -from-kansans-for-life/70116721007/.

66. Rose Conlon, "Kansas governor vetoes 'born-alive' abortion bill, but lawmakers likely have the votes to override," *NPR*, April 14, 2023, https://www.kcur.org/2023-04-14/kansas-governor-vetoes-born-alive -abortion-bill-but-lawmakers-may-have-the-votes-to-override.

67. Rose Conlon, "Kansas governor vetoes 'born-alive' abortion bill, but lawmakers likely have the votes to override," *NPR*, April 14, 2023, https://kansasreflector.com/2023/04/26/kansas-house-overrides -governors-vetoes-of-three-anti-abortion-bills/.

68. Sherman Smith, "Kansas Legislature overrides governor's veto of anti-abortion bill," *Kansas Reflector*, April 26, 2023, https://azmirror .com/2023/04/06/hobbs-vetoes-election-abortion-bills/.

69. 40 Days for Life, "The abortion industry's push to legalize infanticide with abortion survivor Melissa Ohden - PODCAST Season 4, Episode 11," *The 40 Days for Life Podcast*, March 12, 2019, https:// www.40daysforlife.com/en/2019/03/12/the-abortion-industrys-push -to-legalize-infanticide-with-abortion-survivor-melissa-ohden-podcast -season-4-episode-11.

70. Planned Parenthood, "FACT CHECK: So-Called 'Born Alive' is Another Lie To Stigmatize Abortion," January 11, 2023, https:// www.plannedparenthood.org/about-us/newsroom/press-releases /fact-check-so-called-born-alive-is-another-lie-to-stigmatize-abortion-2.

71. 40 Days for Life, "PODCAST #54: Melissa Ohden—meet an abortion survivor," *The 40 Days for Life Podcast*, January 10, 2017, https://www.40daysforlife.com/en/2017/01/10/podcast-54.

72. 40 Days for Life, "The abortion industry's push to legalize infanticide with abortion survivor Melissa Ohden - PODCAST Season 4, Episode 11," *The 40 Days for Life Podcast*, March 12, 2019, https:// www.40daysforlife.com/en/2019/03/12/the-abortion-industrys-push -to-legalize-infanticide-with-abortion-survivor-melissa-ohden-podcast -season-4-episode-11.

73. Charlotte Lozier Institute, "Questions and Answers on Born-Alive Abortion Survivors," January 27, 2023, https://lozierinstitute.org/questions-and-answers-on-born-alive-abortion-survivors/.

74. Heritage Action for America, "Setting the Record Straight on the Born-Alive Abortion Survivors Protection Act: Claims and Responses," March 21, 2019, https://heritageaction.com/blog/setting-the-record-straight-on-the-born-alive-abortion-survivors-protection-act-claims-and-responses.

75. Charlotte Lozier Institute, "Questions and Answers on Born-Alive Abortion Survivors."

76. Population Reference Bureau, "International Data," https://www.prb.org/international/indicator/population/map/country.

77. The Abortion Survivors Network, "Estimated Number of Abortion Survivors," https://abortionsurvivors.org/estimated-number-of-abortion-survivors/.

78. 40 Days for Life, "The abortion industry's push to legalize infanticide with abortion survivor Melissa Ohden - PODCAST Season 4, Episode 11."

79. Wm. Robert Johnston, "Summary of Reported and Estimated Abortions Worldwide, through December 2018," updated December 31, 2018, https://www.johnstonsarchive.net/policy/abortion/wrjp3318.html.

Chapter 4

1. https://www.azquotes.com/quote/373837.

2. Maya Yang, "Man gets life sentence for raping girl, nine, forced to leave Ohio for abortion," *The Guardian*, July 6, 2023, https://www.theguardian.com/world/2023/jul/06/nine-year-old-child-rape-victim-abortion-indiana-ohio-life-sentence.

3. David Folkenflik, Sarah McCammon, "A rape, an abortion, and a one-source story: a child's ordeal becomes national news," *NPR*, July 13, 2022, https://www.npr.org/2022/07/13/1111285143/abortion-10-year-old-raped-ohio.

4. Ibid.

5. Moira Donegan, "She performed an abortion on a 10-year-old rape victim. The right vilified her," *The Guardian*, July 10, 2023, https://www.theguardian.com/commentisfree/2023/jul/10/indiana-abortion-doctor-10-year-old-child-rape.

6. Priscilla K. Coleman, "Abortion and mental health: quantitative synthesis and analysis of research published 1995-2009," September 2011, https://pubmed.ncbi.nlm.nih.gov/21881096/.

7. Allie Griffin, "Man charged with raping, impregnating 10-year-old Ohio girl entered US illegally," *New York Post*, published July 14, 2022, updated July 15, 2022, https://nypost.com/2022/07/14/gershon-fuentes-charged-with-raping-impregnating-ohio-girl-entered-us-illegally/ found via https://nypost.com/2023/07/05/gerson-fuentes-sentenced-to-life-for-raping-9-year-old-girl/.

8. Solcyre Burga, "How a 10-Year-Old Rape Victim Who Traveled for an Abortion Became Part of a Political Firestorm," *Time*, July 15, 2022, https://time.com/6198062/rape-victim-10-abortion-indiana-ohio/.

9. Chelsea Bailey, "Indiana abortion doctor: Caitlin Bernard fined for speaking about 10-year-old," *BBC News*, May 26, 2023, https://www.bbc.com/news/world-us-canada-65714672.

10. Kristi Hofferber, "Hard Cases: Kristi Hofferber," Feminists for Life of America, https://www.feministsforlife.org/hard-cases-kristi-hofferber/.

11. Ibid.

12. Nancy Flanders, "Couple was asked to consider aborting their second baby after older son was diagnosed," Live Action, May 12, 2024, https://www.liveaction.org/news/couple-asked-aborting-second-baby-son-diagnosed/.

13. Ibid.

14. Khalil Shahyd, "The Climate Crisis Is a Reproductive Justice Issue," the Natural Resources Defense Council, May 5, 2022, https://www.nrdc.org/bio/khalil-shahyd/climate-crisis-reproductive-justice-issue.

Chapter 5

1. Joachim I. Krueger Ph.D., "In Defense of Ad Hominem Arguments," *Psychology Today*, May 17, 2024, https://www.psychologytoday.com/us/blog/one-among-many/202405/in-defense-of-ad-hominem-arguments.

2. Ed Mazza, "George Carlin Nailed Conservative Hypocrisy On Abortion More Than 25 Years Ago," May 4, 2022, https://www.huffpost.com/entry/george-carlin-abortion_n_62721f4fe4b0cca6755baf77.

3. George Carlin, "George Carlin SHREDS Republicans in resurfaced megaviral abortion rant: 'They're ANTI-WOMEN,'" Meidas Touch, posted May 4, 2022, https://www.youtube.com/watch?v=hzUGFXKj7hM.

4. Moira Gaul, "Fact Sheet: Pregnancy Centers—Serving Women and Saving Lives (2020 Study)," July 19, 2021, https://lozierinstitute.org/fact-sheet-pregnancy-centers-serving-women-and-saving-lives-2020/.

Chapter 6

1. Michael Foust, "Bill Maher Surprised by Abortion Data: 'Most People Who Are Pro-Life Are Women—I Did Not Know That,'" Crosswalk.com, May 12, 2022, https://www.crosswalk.com/headlines/contributors/michael-foust/bill-maher-surprised-by-abortion-data-most-people-who-are-pro-life-are-women-i-did-not-know-that.html.

2. Will Evans, "When Speeches Come Back To Haunt," *NPR*, October 16, 2008, https://www.npr.org/sections/secretmoney/2008/10/family_research_council.html.

3. 110th Congress, "S.1173 Freedom of Choice Act," April 19, 2007, https://www.congress.gov/bill/110th-congress/senate-bill/1173/text#:~:text=(a)%20Statement%20of%20policy.,or%20health%20of%20the%20woman.

4. Robert P. George, "Obama's Abortion Extremism," October 14, 2008, https://robertpgeorge.com/articles/obamas-abortion-extremism/.

5. Rich Lowry, "Obama the abortion extremist," *Politico*, August 23, 2012, https://www.politico.com/story/2012/08/the-abortion-extremist-080013.

6. Gerald D. Coleman, "A Failure to See: Barack Obama, FOCA & Catholic attitudes about abortion," *America*, February 9, 2009, https://www.americamagazine.org/issue/685/100/failure-see.

7. Osayi Osar-Empokae, "History of the Freedom of Choice Act," Americans United for Life, April 23, 2010, https://aul.org/2010/04/23/history-of-the-freedom-of-choice-act/.

8. Ibid.

9. Anna North, "How the abortion debate moved away from 'safe, legal, and rare,'" *Vox*, October 18, 2019, https://www.vox.com/2019/10/18/20917406/abortion-safe-legal-and-rare-tulsi-gabbard.

10. United States Senate, "Vetoes by President William J. Clinton," https://www.senate.gov/legislative/vetoes/ClintonWJ.htm.

11. United States Senate, "Roll Call Vote 104th Congress, 1st Session," https://www.senate.gov/legislative/LIS/roll_call_votes/vote1041/vote_104_1_00596.htm.

12. United States Senate, "Roll Call Vote 105th Congress, 1st Session," https://www.senate.gov/legislative/LIS/roll_call_votes/vote1051/vote_105_1_00071.htm.

13. Carrie Budoff Brown, "Obama boosts anti-abortion efforts," *Politico*, April 13, 2009, https://www.politico.com/story/2009/04/obama-boosts-anti-abortion-efforts-021158.

14. "Thousands of anti-FOCA postcards delivered to Congress," *Catholic News Agency*, April 5, 2009, https://www.catholicnewsagency.com/news/15574/thousands-of-anti-foca-postcards-delivered-to-congress.

15. Brown, "Obama boosts anti-abortion efforts."

16. Jess Henig, "Ask FactCheck: Freedom of Choice Act," *FactCheck.org*, published February 11, 2009, updated April 30, 2009, https://www.factcheck.org/2009/02/freedom-of-choice-act/.

17. Molly Moorhead, "Nothing to sign; bill has fizzled," *PolitiFact*, June 1, 2012, https://www.politifact.com/truth-o-meter/promises/obameter/promise/501/sign-the-freedom-of-choice-act/.

18. Supreme Court Historical Society, "The Current Court: Justice Amy Coney Barrett," https://supremecourthistory.org/supreme-court-justices/associate-justice-amy-coney-barrett/.

19. Darragh Roche, "Barack Obama Blasted for Not Codifying Roe v. Wade: 'Dem Failure,'" *Newsweek*, June 25, 2022, https://www.newsweek.com/barack-obama-blasted-not-codifying-roe-v-wade-democrat-failure-1719156.

20. David Garrow, "A Look At . . . Roe v. Wade v. Ginsburg: History Lesson for the Judge: What Clinton's Supreme Court Nominee Doesn't Know About Roe," June 20, 1993, https://www.davidgarrow.com/File/DJG%201993%20WashPostOutlookRBGRoe20June.pdf.

21. Michell Ye Hee Lee, "Is the United States one of seven countries that 'allow elective abortions after 20 weeks of pregnancy?'" *The Washington Post*, October 9, 2017, https://www.washingtonpost.com/news/fact-checker/wp/2017/10/09/is-the-united-states-one-of-seven-countries-that-allow-elective-abortions-after-20-weeks-of-pregnancy/.

22. Domenico Montanaro, "Poll: Americans want abortion restrictions, but not as far as red states are going," *NPR*, April 26, 2023, https://www.npr.org/2023/04/26/1171863775/poll-americans-want-abortion-restrictions-but-not-as-far-as-red-states-are-going.

23. Caitlin O'Kane, "New York passes law allowing abortions at any time if mother's health is at risk," *CBS News*, January 24, 2019, https://

www.cbsnews.com/news/new-york-passes-abortion-bill-late-term-if
-mothers-health-is-at-risk-today-2019-01-23/.

24. KFF, "Rate of Legal Abortions per 1,000 Women Aged 15-44 Years by State of Occurrence," https://www.kff.org/womens-health-policy/state-indicator/abortion-rate/?currentTimeframe=0&selectedRows=%7B%22states%22:%7B%22all%22:%7B%7D%7D,%22wrapups%22:%7B%22united-states%22:%7B%7D%7D%7D&sortModel=%7B%22colId%22:%22Abortion%20Rate%22,%22sort%22:%22desc%22%7D.

25. Guttmacher Institute, "State Facts About Abortion: New York," June 2022, https://web.archive.org/web/20230516093811/https://www.guttmacher.org/fact-sheet/state-facts-about-abortion-new-york.

26. Lauren Caruba, "Cynthia Meyer says more black babies are aborted in New York City than born," *PolitiFact*, November 25, 2015, https://www.politifact.com/factchecks/2015/nov/25/cynthia-meyer/cynthia-meyer-says-more-black-babies-are-aborted-n/.

27. Joseph Spector, "Cuomo defends abortion-rights law in New York amid ongoing criticism," *Democrat & Chronicle*, February 5, 2019, https://www.democratandchronicle.com/story/news/politics/albany/2019/02/05/cuomo-defends-abortion-rights-law-amid-ongoing-criticism-trump/2778630002/.

28. Ibid.

29. Sam Sawyer, S.J., "Explainer: What New York's new abortion law does and doesn't do," *America*, January 30, 2019, https://www.americamagazine.org/rha2019.

30. Caroline Kelly, "Rhode Island governor signs abortion protection bill," *CNN*, June 20, 2019, https://www.cnn.com/2019/06/20/politics/rhode-island-governor-signs-abortion-protection-bill/index.html.

31. Vanessa Romo, "Massachusetts Senate Overrides Veto, Passes Law Expanding Abortion Access," *NPR*, December 29, 2020, https://www.npr.org/2020/12/29/951259506/massachusetts-senate-overrides-veto-passes-law-expanding-abortion-access.

32. Kevin J. Jones, "Illinois governor signs 'radical' abortion expansion, but pro-life leaders predict backlash," *Catholic News Agency*, June 13, 2019, https://www.catholicnewsagency.com/news/41539/illinois-governor-signs-radical-abortion-expansion-but-pro-life-leaders-predict-backlash.

33. Caroline Kelly, "GOP Vermont governor to allow abortion rights bill to become law," *CNN*, July 6, 2019, https://www.cnn.com/2019/05/22/politics/vermont-governor-abortion-bill/index.html.

34. Colorado General Assembly, "Reproductive Health Equity Act," 2022, https://leg.colorado.gov/bills/hb22-1279.

35. Caroline Kelly, "Illinois governor signs sweeping abortion protection bill into law," *CNN*, June 12, 2019, https://www.cnn.com/2019/06/12/politics/illinois-governor-signs-abortion-protection-law/index.html.

36. Victoria Colliver, "5 ways California is protecting abortion," *Politico*, September 27, 2022, https://www.politico.com/news/2022/09/27/five-ways-california-is-protecting-abortion-00059090.

37. Gabe Stern, "Nevada Republican governor approves abortion protections in cross-party move," Associated Press, "May 31, 2023, https://apnews.com/article/nevada-abortion-republican-governor-joe-lombardo-83032873a48a8916b7d030191d095bc4.

38. Hannah Metzger, "Colorado is now among strongest states for abortion protections," *Colorado Politics*, published May 21, 2023, updated July 10, 2023, https://www.coloradopolitics.com/legislature/colorado-abortion-leader/article_5fa68358-f58e-11ed-adc0-9b455b113b28.html.

39. Steve Karnowski, "Minnesota governor signs broad abortion rights bill into law," Associated Press, January 31, 2023, https://apnews.com/article/abortion-politics-minnesota-state-government-timothy-walz-11c3b1d5269c929e442b979ff1bac73b.

40. Richard Doerflinger, M.A., "Lies, Damn Lies, and the Women's Health Protection Act," Charlotte Lozier Institute, October 6, 2021, https://lozierinstitute.org/lies-damn-lies-and-the-womens-health-protection-act/.

41. Rachel M. Cohen, "There's a bipartisan bill to codify Roe — and abortion rights groups can't stand it," *Vox*, August 22, 2022, https://www.vox.com/policy-and-politics/2022/8/22/23306142/kaine-collins-codify-roe-abortion-congress.

42. Doerflinger, "Lies, Damn Lies, and the Women's Health Protection Act."

43. Liz Zhou, "The Senate's doomed vote on abortion rights, explained," *Vox*, May 11, 2022, https://www.vox.com/2022/5/11/23065959/senate-abortion-vote-womens-health-protection-act.

44. Doerflinger, "Lies, Damn Lies, and the Women's Health Protection Act."

45. Christian Mysliwiec, Melanie Israel, "Understanding the Left's Plan to Codify Roe v. Wade Into Law," the Heritage Foundation,

December 10, 2021, https://www.heritage.org/life/commentary/under standing-the-lefts-plan-codify-roe-v-wade-law.

46. Doerflinger, "Lies, Damn Lies, and the Women's Health Protection Act."

47. 117th Congress, "H.R.3755 - Women's Health Protection Act of 2021," June 8, 2021, https://www.congress.gov/bill/117th-congress /house-bill/3755/actions.

48. Zhou, "The Senate's doomed vote on abortion rights, explained," https://www.vox.com/2022/5/11/23065959/senate-abortion-vote -womens-health-protection-act.

49. The White House, "Statement from President Biden on the Senate Vote on the Women's Health Protection Act," May 11, 2022, https:// www.whitehouse.gov/briefing-room/statements-releases/2022/05/11 /statement-from-president-biden-on-the-senate-vote-on-the-womens -health-protection-act/.

Chapter 7

1. Robert Siegel and Connor Donevan, "'Hemingway Didn't Say That' (And Neither Did Twain Or Kafka)," *NPR*, April 4, 2017, https://www.npr.org/2017/04/04/522581148/hemingway-didnt-say -that-and-neither-did-twain-or-kafka.

2. Caroline Kitchener, "This Texas teen wanted an abortion. She now has twins." *The Washington Post*, June 20, 2022, https:// www.washingtonpost.com/politics/2022/06/20/texas-abortion -law-teen-mom/.

3. Ibid.

4. Caroline Kitchener, "An abortion ban made them teen parents," *The Washington Post*, August 1, 2023, https://www.washingtonpost.com/ politics/interactive/2023/texas-abortion-law-teen-parents/.

5. Ibid.

6. Ibid.

7. Cassy Fiano-Chesser, "The Turnaway Study Takedown: Video debunks 'research' claiming women suffer when denied abortion," Live Action, September 28, 2022, https://www.liveaction.org/news/ turnaway-study-takedown-video-debunks-denied-abortion/.

8. Kitchener, "An abortion ban made them teen parents."

9. Kitchener, "This Texas teen wanted an abortion. She now has twins."

10. Kitchener, "An abortion ban made them teen parents."

11. Jenny Goldsberry, "WATCH: Rep. Porter says abortion and inflation 'reinforce each other,'" *Washington Examiner*, May 12, 2022, https://www.washingtonexaminer.com/news/watch-rep-porter-says -abortion-and-inflation-reinforce-each-other.

12. Tom Tillison, "Panel laughs as MSNBC guest wants to 'make sweet love' to SCOTUS leaker and 'joyfully abort our fetus,'" *American Wire*, May 9, 2022, https://americanwirenews.com/panel-laughs-as-msnbc-guest-wants-to-make-sweet-love-to-scotus-leaker-and-joyfully-abort-our-fetus/.

13. Motherboard, *Vice*, May 3, 2022, https://twitter.com/ motherboard/status/1521511916912488448?

14. Jason Koebler, "Anarchist Collective Shares Instructions to Make DIY Abortion Pills," *Vice*, May 3, 2022, https://www .vice.com/en/article/qjby4b/anarchist-collective-shares-instructions -to-make-diy-abortion-pills.

15. Tiffany Green and Jenny Higgins, "UW professors: Dobbs forced at least 1,500 unintended births, causing harm to Wisconsin communities," *Wisconsin State Journal*, December 14, 2023, https:// madison.com/opinion/column/uw-professors-dobbs-forced-at-least -1-500-unintended-births-causing-harm-to-wisconsin-communities/ article_5ca609da-9912-11ee-8970-43a390d8a11c.html.

16. Ibid.

17. Townhall, May 3, 2022, https://twitter.com/townhallcom/ status/1521562870261202945.

18. Valerie Baron, "Dobbs Is Dangerous, Especially in an Era of Climate Change," NRDC, July 6, 2022, https://www.nrdc.org/bio/ valerie-baron/dobbs-dangerous-especially-era-climate-change.

19. The White House, "Remarks by Vice President Harris on the Supreme Court Decision to Overturn Roe V. Wade," June 24, 2022, https://www.whitehouse.gov/briefing-room/speeches-remarks/2022 /06/24/remarks-by-vice-president-harris-on-the-supreme-court -decision-to-overturn-roe-v-wade/#:~:text=In%20holding%20that%20 it%20is,the%20right%20to%20interracial%20marriage.

20. Nicholas Kristof, "America Is Losing Religious Faith," *The New York Times*, August 23, 2023, https://www.nytimes.com/2023/08/23/ opinion/christianity-america-religion-secular.html.

21. Christina Cauterucci, "The Religious Left Has Found Its Mission," *Slate*, November 7, 2022, https://slate.com/news-and-politics

/2022/11/after-dobbs-abortion-bans-pro-choice-religious-groups-and
-clergy-are-politically-active.html.

22. Ibid.

23. U.S. Department of Justice, Civil Rights Division, "Recent Cases on Violence Against Reproductive Health Care Providers," https://www.justice.gov/crt/recent-cases-violence-against-reproductive -health-care-providers.

24. Brandon Gillespie, "Reporter calls for violence against pro-lifers, says they shouldn't have 'peace or safety' until they're dead," *Fox News*, May 9, 2022, https://www.foxnews.com/media/ reporter-violence-pro-lifers-peace-safety-dead.

25. Jessica Chasmar, "More than 100 pro-life orgs, churches attacked since Dobbs leak," *Fox News*, October 20, 2022, https://www .foxnews.com/politics/100-pro-life-orgs-churches-attacked-dobbs-leak.

26. Sarah D., "Hillary Clinton doesn't want to 'accept a future in which our daughters and granddaughters have fewer rights than we did' (if they aren't aborted)," *Twitchy*, May 11, 2022, https://twitchy.com/ sarahd-313035/2022/05/11/hillary-clinton-doesnt-want-to-accept-a -future-in-which-our-daughters-and-granddaughters-have-fewer-rights -than-we-did-if-they-arent-aborted/.

27. The White House, "Remarks by President Biden Before Air Force One Departure," May 3, 2022, https://www.whitehouse.gov /briefing-room/speeches-remarks/2022/05/03/remarks-by-president -biden-before-air-force-one-departure-15/#:~:text=I%20mean%2 C%20so%20the%20idea,I%20think%2C%20goes%20way%20 overboard.

28. "Reactions to the Supreme Court overturning Roe v. Wade," Reuters, June 26, 2022, https://www.reuters.com/world/us/ reactions-us-supreme-court-overturning-roe-v-wade-abortion-land mark-2022-06-24/.

29. Brian Flood, "Former CBS reporter becomes Planned Parenthood's 'news content' director," *Fox News*, April 25, 2022, https:// www.foxnews.com/media/former-cbs-reporter-becomes-planned -parenthoods-news-content-director.

30. Kate Smith, originally accessed at https://twitter.com/ byKateSmith/status/1521297279306633221.

31. Joseph A. Wulfsohn, "CBS News reporter quits, says she can now 'be candid' about her support for 'abortion rights,'" *Fox News*,

July 15, 2021, https://www.foxnews.com/media/cbs-news-kate-smith
-abortion-rights.

32. Alexandra DeSanctis, "Former CBS News 'Reporter' Kate
Smith Joins Planned Parenthood," *National Review*, April 25, 2022,
https://www.nationalreview.com/corner/former-cbs-news-reporter
-kate-smith-joins-planned-parenthood/.

Chapter 8

1. *AZ Quotes*, https://www.azquotes.com/quotes/topics/pills.html.
2. Ahmed Aboulenein, "U.S. FDA allows abortion pills to be sold at
retail pharmacies," Reuters, January 4, 2023, https://www.reuters.com/
world/us/us-fda-says-abortion-pills-can-be-sold-retail-pharmacies-new
-york-times-reports-2023-01-03/.
3. Pam Belluck, "CVS and Walgreens Plan to Offer Abortion Pills
Where Abortion Is Legal," *The New York Times*, January 5, 2023, https://
www.nytimes.com/2023/01/05/health/abortion-pills-cvs-walgreens
.html.
4. "Rite Aid to dispense abortion pill in a limited number of
stores," Reuters, January 19, 2023, https://www.reuters.com/world/us/
rite-aid-dispense-abortion-pill-limited-number-stores-2023-01-19/.
5. Alice Miranda Ollstein and Lauren Gardner, "Pharmacies
begin dispensing abortion pills," *Politico*, October 26, 2023,
https://www.politico.com/news/2023/10/06/pharmacies-begin
-dispensing-abortion-pills-00120397.
6. Amy Quinton, "Unsafe Feeding Methods Spiked During
Infant Formula Shortage," UC Davis, June 27, 2023, https://
www.ucdavis.edu/health/news/unsafe-feeding-methods-spiked
-during-infant-formula-shortage.
7. 40 Days for Life, "CVS and Walgreens to Replace Planned
Parenthood as America's Biggest Abortion Chains—PODCAST Season
8, Episode 4," *The 40 Days for Life Podcast*, January 24, 2023, https://
www.40daysforlife.com/en/pharmacy_abortions.
8. Clare Cain Miller and Margot Sanger-Katz, "What is mifepristone
and how is it used?" *The New York Times*, June 13, 2024, https://www
.nytimes.com/2024/06/13/us/politics/what-is-mifepristone.html.
9. Ollstein and Gardner, "Pharmacies begin dispensing abortion
pills."
10. Medline Plus, "Misoprostol," https://medlineplus.gov/druginfo/
meds/a689009.html.

11. Marjorie Dannenfelser, "Take Dangerous Abortion Drugs Off The Market," *Newsweek*, January 13, 2023, https://www.newsweek.com/take-dangerous-abortion-drugs-off-market-opinion-1773043.

12. Jacqueline Howard, "Some major pharmacies are planning to dispense abortion pills, but not in every state," CNN, January 5, 2023, https://www.cnn.com/2023/01/04/health/fda-abortion-pills-pharmacies-xpn/index.html.

13. U.S. FDA, "Information about Mifepristone for Medical Termination of Pregnancy Through Ten Weeks Gestation," https://www.fda.gov/drugs/postmarket-drug-safety-information-patients-and-providers/information-about-mifepristone-medical-termination-pregnancy-through-ten-weeks-gestation.

14. Rachel K. Jones, Elizabeth Nash, Lauren Cross, Jesse Philbin, Marielle Kirstein, "Medication Abortion Now Accounts for More Than Half of All US Abortions," published February 24, 2022, updated December 1, 2022, https://www.guttmacher.org/article/2022/02/medication-abortion-now-accounts-more-half-all-us-abortion.

15. Wm. Robert Johnston, "Historical abortion statistics, United States," updated February 24, 2024, https://www.johnstonsarchive.net/policy/abortion/ab-unitedstates.html.

16. Thomas Jipping, "Chemical Abortion Is Next Pro-Life Battlefield," the Heritage Foundation, July 29, 2022, https://www.heritage.org/life/commentary/chemical-abortion-next-pro-life-battlefield.

17. Johnston, "Historical abortion statistics, United States."

18. Anna North, "America's first generic abortion pill, explained," *Vox*, August 20, 2019, https://www.vox.com/identities/2019/8/20/20750226/abortion-pill-mifepristone-pregnancy-genbiopro-mifeprex-generic.

19. Carole Novielli, "The abortion industry is making a killing from abortion pill sales," Live Action, September 16, 2020, https://www.liveaction.org/news/industry-making-killing-abortion-pill-sales/.

20. North, "America's first generic abortion pill, explained."

21. ANSIRH, "The average out-of-pocket cost for medication abortion is increasing, new study confirms," University of California San Francisco, April 11, 2022, https://www.ansirh.org/research/research/average-out-pocket-cost-medication-abortion-increasing-new-study-confirms https://www.ansirh.org/research/research/average-out-pocket-cost-medication-abortion-increasing-new-study-confirms found via https://www.liveaction.org/news/industry-profits-abortion-pill-skyrocket-taxpayer-funding/.

22. Hannah Levintova, "The Abortion Pill's Secret Money Men," *Mother Jones*, March/April 2023, https://www.motherjones.com/politics/2023/01/abortion-pill-mifepristone-mifeprex-roe-dobbs-private-equity/.

23. Ibid.

24. Planned Parenthood, "Abortion Options," https://cdn.plannedparenthood.org/uploads/filer_public/ce/60/ce60c6e3-8528-410f-9bb9-803f142ff2a2/pes_52_-_abortion_options_english.pdf.

25. Abby Johnson, "Tonsillectomy," October 23, 2011, https://abbyj.com/tonsillectomy/.

26. Ibid.

27. Mayo Clinic, "Medical Abortion," June 28, 2024, mayoclinic.org/tests-procedures/medical-abortion/about/pac-20394687.

28. Emma Specter, "What Is It Like to Have a Medication Abortion? 5 People Share Their Stories," *Vogue*, November 13, 2022, https://www.vogue.com/article/medication-abortion-5-people-share-their-stories.

29. Charlotte Lozier Institute, "Fact Sheet: Risks and Complications of Chemical Abortion," August 23, 2023, https://lozierinstitute.org/fact-sheet-risks-and-complications-of-chemical-abortion/.

30. Mayo Clinic, "Medical Abortion."

31. John Burger, "Letting pharmacies dispense abortion irresponsible, says doctor," *Aleteia*, January 6, 2023, https://aleteia.org/2023/01/06/letting-pharmacies-dispense-abortion-irresponsible-says-doctor/.

32. Maria Wiering, "Despite growing use, abortion pill not 'safer than Tylenol' and carries serious risks, including trauma of flushing a baby down the toilet, pro-life experts say," *Our Sunday Visitor*, May 24, 2023, https://www.oursundayvisitor.com/despite-growing-use-abortion-pill-not-safer-than-tylenol-and-carries-serious-risks-including-trauma-of-flushing-a-baby-down-the-toilet-pro-life-experts-say/.

33. Ibid.

34. Charlotte Lozier Institute, "Fact Sheet: Risks and Complications of Chemical Abortion."

35. Shefali Luthra, "Medication abortion is the nation's future. What does it feel like?" *19th News*, May 23, 2022, https://19thnews.org/2022/05/medication-abortion-pill-self-managed-home-experience/.

36. U.S. FDA, "Questions and Answers on Mifepristone for Medical Termination of Pregnancy Through Ten Weeks Gestation," https://www.fda.gov/drugs/postmarket-drug-safety-information-patients-and

-providers/questions-and-answers-mifepristone-medical-termination
-pregnancy-through-ten-weeks-gestation.

37. Sheena Goodyear, "RU-486: What you need to know about the recently approved abortion pill," CBC, published July 30, 2015, updated July 31, 2015, https://www.cbc.ca/news/canada/ru-486-what-you-need -to-know-about-the-recently-approved-abortion-pill-1.3173657.

38. Sally Murray and Eric Wooltorton, "Septic shock after medical abortions with mifepristone (Mifeprex, RU 486) and misoprostol," CMAJ, August 30, 2005, https://www.ncbi.nlm.nih.gov/pmc/articles/ PMC1188182/.

39. Michael Martinez, "San Francisco bans Happy Meals with toys," CNN, November 9, 2010, https://www.cnn.com/2010/US/11/09/ california.fast.food.ban/index.html.

40. Joe Bukuras, "Pregnant woman given abortion pill by mistake; Nevada CVS fined $10,000," *Catholic News Agency*, October 10, 2023, https://www.catholicnewsagency.com/news/255633/nevada-cvs-gave -pregnant-woman-abortion-pill-fined-10000-dollars.

41. Ibid.

42. Ibid.

43. Sawdah Bhaimiya, "A woman who was accidentally given abortion pills by a pharmacy when she was undergoing IVF said her plans to have a big family were shattered," *Business Insider*, October 7, 2023, https://www.businessinsider.com/woman-accidentally-given-abortion -pills-cvs-pharmacy-ending-pregnancy-2023-10.

44. Andrea Becker and Rachel E. Gross, "The 'Abortion Pill' Is Used for So Much More Than Abortions," *Slate*, July 6, 2022, https:// slate.com/technology/2022/07/roe-wade-abortion-health-care-crisis -misoprostol-mifepristone-d-and-c.html.

45. Bhaimiya, "A woman who was accidentally given abortion pills by a pharmacy when she was undergoing IVF said her plans to have a big family were shattered."

46. David C. Reardon, Ph.D., "Hidden Epidemic: Nearly 70% of Abortions Are Coerced, Unwanted or Inconsistent With Women's Preferences," Charlotte Lozier Institute, May 15, 2023, https:// lozierinstitute.org/hidden-epidemic-nearly-70-of-abortions-are-coerced -unwanted-or-inconsistent-with-womens-preferences/.

47. Dr. Daniel Grossman, "Texas' abortion crisis proves the abortion pill needs to be in every drug store," *NBC News*, September 9, 2021,

https://www.nbcnews.com/think/opinion/texas-abortion-crisis-proves-abortion-pill-needs-be-every-drug-ncna1278829.

48. David C. Reardon, Ph.D.; Donna Harrison, M.D.; Ingrid Skop, M.D., FACOG; Christina A. Cirucci, M.D.; James Studnicki, Sc.D., MPH, MBA, "Overlooked Dangers of Mifepristone, the FDA's Reduced REMS, and Self-Managed Abortion Policies: Unwanted Abortions, Unnecessary Abortions, Unsafe Abortions," Charlotte Lozier Institute, December 16, 2021, https://lozierinstitute.org/overlooked-dangers-of-mifepristone-the-fdas-reduced-rems-and-self-managed-abortion-policies-unwanted-abortions-unnecessary-abortions-unsafe-abortions/.

49. David C. Reardon, "Coercive abortions are at the heart of the FDA abortion pill case," *The Hill*, August 27, 2023, https://thehill.com/opinion/healthcare/4169247-coercive-abortions-are-at-the-heart-of-the-fda-abortion-pill-case/.

50. Rob Mackay, "Police: Florida man secretly slipped pregnant girlfriend abortion pill," *Fox13 News Seattle*, May 16, 2013, https://www.fox13seattle.com/news/police-florida-man-secretly-slipped-pregnant-girlfriend-abortion-pill.

51. Mark Osborne, "Former doctor who slipped abortion drug into girlfriend's tea sentenced to 3 years in prison," *ABC News*, May 19, 2018, https://abcnews.go.com/US/doctor-slipped-abortion-drug-girlfriends-tea-sentenced-years/story?id=55280357.

52. "Man Gets 22 Years in Prison for Slipping Abortion Pill Into Pregnant Girlfriend's Drink," *Inside Edition*, October 11, 2018, https://www.insideedition.com/man-gets-22-years-prison-slipping-abortion-pill-pregnant-girlfriends-drink-47528.

53. Tomoki Miyasaka, "Suspect admits to making teen take unapproved abortion pills," *The Asahi Shimbun*, February 23, 2021, https://www.asahi.com/ajw/articles/14213943.

54. Michael Mahar, "Schaghticoke man accused of causing miscarriage," *News10 Albany*, published July 5, 2023, updated July 6, 2023, https://www.news10.com/news/crime/schaghticoke-man-accused-of-causing-miscarriage/.

55. Lauren Aratani, "Texas man faces charges for allegedly slipping abortion drug in wife's drink," *The Guardian*, November 14, 2022, https://www.theguardian.com/us-news/2022/nov/14/texas-mason-herring-abortion-drug-wife-drink-criminal-charges.

56. Carrie N. Baker, "Abortion Pills in Your Medicine Cabinet? Advance Provision Medication to End Early Pregnancies," *Ms.*, December

14, 2021, https://msmagazine.com/2021/12/14/abortion-pill-end-early
-pregnancy-at-home/.

57. 40 Days for Life, "The Doctor Will See You...in Court—
PODCAST Season 9, Episode 18," *The 40 Days for Life Podcast*, April
30, 2024, https://www.40daysforlife.com/en/dr-borrillo-podcast.

58. Steve Karlen, "Outside the Box," *Day 41*, Summer 2018.

59. Ibid.

60. Dr. George Delgado, "A Second Chance at Choice," *Day 41*,
Winter 2021–22.

61. Ibid.

62. Heartbeat International, "A Last Chance to Choose Life,"
https://www.heartbeatinternational.org/our-work/apr.

63. Charlotte Lozier Institute, "Abortion Pill Reversal: A Record
of Safety and Efficacy," September 24, 2021, https://lozierinstitute.org/
abortion-pill-reversal-a-record-of-safety-and-efficacy/.

64. Dr. George Delgado, "Written Testimony of George Delgado,
M.D., F.A.A.F.P., in Support of Colorado Abortion Pill Reversal Bill,"
Charlotte Lozier Institute, February 16, 2017, https://lozierinstitute.
org/written-testimony-of-george-delgado-m-d-f-a-a-f-p-in-support-of-
colorado-abortion-pill-reversal-bill/.

65. Dr. George Delgado, "Written Testimony of George Delgado,
M.D., F.A.A.F.P., in Support of Colorado Abortion Pill Reversal Bill,"
Charlotte Lozier Institute, February 16, 2017, https://lozierinstitute.
org/abortion-pill-reversal-a-record-of-safety-and-efficacy/.

66. https://www.vice.com/en/article/kz44py/study-on-medication-
abortion-reversal-halted-because-of-safety-concerns.

67. Charlotte Lozier Institute, "Abortion Pill Reversal: A Record of
Safety and Efficacy."

68. Abortion Pill Reversal, "FAQ," https://www.abortionpillreversal
.com/abortion-pill-reversal/faq.

69. Ibid.

Chapter 9

1. https://www.azquotes.com/quote/71673.

Chapter 10

1. *The Joe Rogan Experience*, Episode #2115, Aired March 7, 2024.
Quote at 2:27:17.

2. Paul McHugh, "Transgenderism: A Pathogenic Meme," *Public Discourse*, June 10, 2015, https://www.thepublicdiscourse.com/2015/06/15145/.

3. Ibid.

4. Nolan D. McCaskill, "What Castro meant when he said trans women need access to abortions," *Politico*, June 27, 2019, https://www.politico.com/story/2019/06/27/julian-castro-debate-abortion-1385950.

5. Ibid.

6. 40 Days for Life, "A Pro-Choicer Admits Abortion Is Murder—PODCAST Season 9, Episode 17," *The 40 Days for Life Podcast*, April 22, 2024, https://www.youtube.com/watch?v=MiRXzhp-IR8.

7. Jeremy Shaw, M.D., August 24, 2023, https://x.com/jeremy shawmd/status/1694840931743051778?s=66&t=O3Fapd l94O7aJU6FGs0gxA Found via https://www.spiked-online.com/2023/08/29/no-transwomen-should-not-have-abortions/amp/.

8. Ann Furedi, "No, transwomen should not have abortions," *Spiked*, August 29, 2023, https://www.spiked-online.com/2023/08/29/no-transwomen-should-not-have-abortions/amp/.

Chapter 11

1. https://www.abrahamlincolnonline.org/lincoln/speeches/house.htm.

2. American Battlefield Trust, "Civil War Casualties," published November 16, 2012, updated September 15, 2023, https://www.battlefields.org/learn/articles/civil-war-casualties.

3. Alexi McCammond, Andrew Solender, "The big scrub," *Axios*, August 31, 2022, https://www.axios.com/2022/08/31/republicans-midterms.

4. Sahil Kapur, "GOP strategists urge congressional candidates to campaign against a national abortion ban," *NBC News*, November 8, 2023, https://www.nbcnews.com/politics/congress/republicans-urge-congress-candidates-oppose-national-abortion-ban-rcna124253.

5. Julie Tsirkin, Kate Santaliz, Brennan Leach, and Liz Brown-Kaiser, "Republicans are trying to find a new term for 'pro-life' to stave off more electoral losses," *NBC News*, September 7, 2023, https://www.nbcnews.com/politics/congress/republicans-try-find-new-term-life-stave-electoral-losses-rcna103924.

6. Ibid.

7. Kevin Cramer, "Sen. Cramer Receives Life Protector Award from North Dakota Right to Life," January 19, 2023, https://www.cramer.senate.gov/news/press-releases/sen-cramer-receives-life-protector-award-from-north-dakota-right-to-life

8. Allan Smith, "Trump criticizes Republicans pushing abortion bans with no exceptions: 'You're not going to win,'" *NBC News*, September 16, 2023, https://www.nbcnews.com/politics/donald-trump/trump-bring-country-together-abortion-meet-the-press-rcna105311.

9. Gallup, "Abortion," https://news.gallup.com/poll/1576/abortion.aspx.

10. Ibid.

11. Ibid.

12. Ibid.

13. Caroline Vakil and Nathaniel Weixel, "Republicans struggle for way out of abortion quagmire," *The Hill*, November 9, 2023, https://thehill.com/homenews/campaign/4303069-republicans-abortion-election-2023-ohio-losses/.

14. Chris Good, "Mitt Romney, the Abortion and Contraception Moderate in New TV Ad," *ABC News*, October 17, 2012, https://abcnews.go.com/blogs/politics/2012/10/mitt-romney-the-abortion-and-contraception-moderate-in-new-tv-ad.

15. John Dickerson, "Why Romney Never Saw It Coming," *Slate*, November 9, 2012, https://slate.com/news-and-politics/2012/11/why-romney-was-surprised-to-lose-his-campaign-had-the-wrong-numbers-bad-assumptions-and-underestimated-barack-obamas-campaign-team.html.

16. The Editors, "Take the Long View on the Fight for Life," *National Review*, November 8, 2023, https://www.nationalreview.com/2023/11/take-the-long-view-on-the-fight-for-life/ Found via https://washingtonstand.com/commentary/the-left-wants-you-to-despair-after-tuesdays-election-dont.

17. United States Senate, "Roll Call Vote, 108th Congress, 2nd Session," July 14, 2004, https://www.senate.gov/legislative/LIS/roll_call_votes/vote1082/vote_108_2_00155.htm#position.

18. The Editors, "Take the Long View on the Fight for Life."

19. Domenico Montanaro, "Poll: Americans want abortion restrictions, but not as far as red states are going," *NPR*, April 26, 2023, https://www.npr.org/2023/04/26/1171863775/poll-americans-want-abortion-restrictions-but-not-as-far-as-red-states-are-going.

20. Jeff Diamant, Besheer Mohamed, and Rebecca Leppert, "What the data says about abortion in the U.S.," Pew Research Center, March 25, 2024, https://www.pewresearch.org/short-reads/2023/01/11/what-the-data-says-about-abortion-in-the-u-s-2/.

21. Carrie Sheffield, "Graham's bill would ban very few abortions — and other ways it doesn't help the GOP," *NBC News*, September 15, 2022, https://www.nbcnews.com/think/opinion/grahams-15-week-abortion-ban-bill-is-deadweight-around-gop-neck-rcna47974.

22. Will Weissert, Michelle L. Price, "Pence calls for 2024 GOP candidates to back a 15-week federal abortion ban," *PBS*, June 23, 2023, https://www.pbs.org/newshour/politics/pence-calls-for-2024-gop-candidates-to-back-a-15-week-federal-abortion-ban.

23. Caroline Vakil and Julia Manchester, "Republicans divided over 15-week abortion ban ahead of 2024," *The Hill*, July 4, 2023, https://thehill.com/homenews/campaign/4076616-republicans-divided-over-15-week-abortion-ban-ahead-of-2024/.

24. Sara Burnett, "DeSantis said he would support a 15-week abortion ban, after avoiding a direct answer for months," Associated Press, October 3, 2023, https://apnews.com/article/abortion-republicans-desantis-trump-bdccde60987da99018bf3abcbafedea0.

25. Ed Kilgore, "Will Voters Buy Youngkin's 15-Week Abortion-Ban Gambit?" *New York*, October 26, 2023, https://nymag.com/intelligencer/2023/10/will-voters-buy-youngkins-15-week-abortion-ban-gambit.html.

26. Charles A. "Chuck" Donovan and Angelina B. Nguyen, "U.S. abortion policy shouldn't emulate China or North Korea. We should be more like Europe." *USA Today*, July 27, 2021, https://www.usatoday.com/story/opinion/2021/07/27/mississippi-abortion-law-mirrors-commonsense-legislation-europe/8060772002/?gnt-cfr=1.

27. Right to Life, "What are the abortion time limits in EU countries?" https://righttolife.org.uk/what-are-the-abortion-time-limits-in-eu-countries.

28. Pauline Turuban, "How abortion rights in Switzerland compare internationally," SWI, July 7, 2022, https://www.swissinfo.ch/eng/society/how-abortion-rights-in-switzerland-compare-internationally/47725444.

29. Abraham Lincoln, "House Divided Speech," June 16, 1858, Mark E. Neely Jr., *The Abraham Lincoln Encyclopedia*, New York: Da Capo Press, 1982, https://www.nps.gov/liho/learn/historyculture/housedivided.htm.

30. Nathaniel Weixel, "Haley on abortion: 'We don't need to divide America,'" *The Hill*, November 8, 2023,https://thehill.com/policy/healthcare/4301213-haley-on-abortion-we-dont-need-to-divide-america/.

31. Tsirkin, Santaliz, Leach, and Brown-Kaiser, "Republicans are trying to find a new term for 'pro-life' to stave off more electoral losses."

32. *The New York Times*, "Election 2010," https://archive.nytimes.com/www.nytimes.com/elections/2010/results/florida.html?src=tp.

33. *The New York Times*, "Florida Election Results," December 17, 2014, https://www.nytimes.com/elections/2014/florida-elections.

34. *Politico*, "Florida Governor Election Results, 2018," https://www.politico.com/election-results/2018/florida/governor/.

35. Elise Elder, "DeSantis wins 2022 Florida governor's race by largest margin in 40 years," WUFT, November 9, 2022, https://www.wuft.org/news/2022/11/08/desantis-wins-2022-florida-governors-race-by-largest-margin-in-40-years/.

36. Arek Sarkissian, "DeSantis says Florida will 'expand pro-life protections' after Supreme Court ruling," *Politico*, June 24, 2022, https://www.politico.com/news/2022/06/24/gov-ron-desantis-calls-to-expand-pro-life-protection-after-historic-abortion-ruling-00042333.

37. Jo Yurcaba, "DeSantis signs 'Don't Say Gay' expansion and gender-affirming care ban," *NBC News*, May 17, 2023, https://www.nbcnews.com/nbc-out/out-politics-and-policy/desantis-signs-dont-say-gay-expansion-gender-affirming-care-ban-rcna84698.

38. Elder, "DeSantis wins 2022 Florida governor's race by largest margin in 40 years."

39. Elizabeth Bruenig, "Why Pro-Lifers Should Sweat the Details of Abortion Penalties," *The New Republic*, April 10, 2015, https://newrepublic.com/article/121511/rand-paul-raises-questions-about-abortion.

40. W. James Antle III, "The lessons of Rand Paul's pro-life victory," *The Week*, April 10, 2015, https://theweek.com/articles/549007/lessons-rand-pauls-prolife-victory.

41. Alexandra Villareal, "Abortion Becomes Final Debate Flashpoint With 'Late-Term' Question," *NBC4 Washington*, published October 20, 2016, updated October 21, 2016, https://www.nbcwashington.com/news/local/trump-condemns-ninth-month-abortions-debate-experts-respond-clinton-late-term/113118/.

42. Students for Life of America, "Online Survey of 18-34-year-old Registered Voters Nationally," January 5-11, 2022, https://www

.instituteforprolifeadvancement.org/wp-content/uploads/2022/01/
SFLAAbPoll2022Topline-final-FULL-PDF.pdf.

43. Ibid.

44. Michael A. Cohen, "Voters Rejected Wackjobs and Rewarded Competence in State Elections," *Yahoo! Finance*, November 14, 2022, https://uk.finance.yahoo.com/news/voters-rejected-wackjobs-rewarded-competence-180749766.html.

45. John F. Harris, "The 2022 Election Was Almost Normal," *Politico*, November 9, 2022, https://www.politico.com/news/magazine /2022/11/09/the-2022-election-was-almost-normal-00066036.

46. FDOT, "ICYMI: Governor Ron DeSantis Announces Emergency Road and Bridge Repairs to Pine Island Completed Ahead of Schedule," October 5, 2022, https://www.fdot.gov/info/co/news /2022/10052022.

47. Ryan Kruger, "A rebuilt bridge could play a big role in DeSantis campaign," *Fox4*, May 25, 2023, https://www.fox4now .com/news/local-news/lee-county/a-rebuilt-bridge-could-play-a -big-role-in-desantis-campaign.

48. Nada Tawfik, "Ron DeSantis: How the Republican governor conquered Florida," *BBC*, November 11, 2022, https://www.bbc.com/ news/world-us-canada-63565224.

Chapter 12

1. Leia Idliby, "Whoopi Goldberg Darkly Recalls 'Tripping Over Women' Giving Themselves Abortions in 'Public Bathrooms,'" *Mediaite*, May 3, 2022, https://www.mediaite.com/tv/whoopi-goldberg-darkly -recalls-tripping-over-women-giving-themselves-abortions-in-public -bathrooms/.

2. *Mission: Impossible*, "'They're dead, they're all dead!'" Boxoffice Movie Scenes, posted July 17, 2022, https://www.youtube.com/watch ?v=2vz94YdDQUo.

3. Democracy Now, "'Women Will Die Because of This': Planned Parenthood on Trump Signing Anti-Abortion Global Gag Rule," PBS SoCal, January 24, 2017,https://www.kcet.org/shows/democracy-now/ clip/women-will-die-because-of-this-planned-parenthood-on-trump -signing-anti-abortion-global-gag-rule.

4. Lindsey Wahowiak, "Reproductive health comes under attack by Congress, new president: Threat to health," *The Nation's Health*, April 2017, https://www.thenationshealth.org/content/47/2/1.1.

5. Ibid.

6. Mercury News and East Bay Times editorial boards, "Editorial: Women will die because of Texas abortion law decision," *The Mercury News*, September 4, 2021, https://www.mercurynews.com/2021/09/04/ editorial-texas-abortion/.

7. Emily Canal, "Defunding Planned Parenthood Would Put 900,000 Women's Lives At Risk Every Year," January 5, 2016, https://www.forbes.com/sites/emilycanal/2015/12/09/defunding -planned-parenthood-would-put-900000-womens-lives-at-risk-every -year/?sh=48765cd557ec.

8. Michelle Ye Hee Lee, "The repeated, misleading claim that Planned Parenthood 'provides' mammograms," October 2, 2015, https://www.washingtonpost.com/news/fact-checker/wp/2015/10/02/ the-repeated-misleading-claim-that-planned-parenthood-provides -mammograms/.

9. Swann Arp Adams, Ph.D., et al., "Is Availability of Mammography Services at Federally Qualified Health Centers Associated with Breast Cancer Mortality-to-Incidence Ratios? An Ecological Analysis," *Journal of Women's Health*, November 1, 2015, https://www.ncbi.nlm.nih.gov/ pmc/articles/PMC4808280/.

10. "Why Roe v. Wade must be defended," *The Lancet*, May 14, 2022, https://www.thelancet.com/journals/lancet/article/PIIS0140-6736 (22)00870-4/fulltext.

11. Lorraine Longhi, "Sisolak reaffirms Nevada abortion rights after SCOTUS ruling," *Las Vegas Review-Journal*, June 24, 2022, https://www.reviewjournal.com/news/politics-and-government/nevada/ sisolak-reaffirms-nevada-abortion-rights-after-scotus-ruling-2597984/.

12. Dr. Liz Lyster, "My thoughts on the recent Supreme Court decision that overturned Roe v. Wade," Dr. Liz MD, July 6, 2022, https:// web.archive.org/web/20220810080617/https://drlizmd.com/blog-my -thoughts-on-the-recent-supreme-court-decision-that-overturned-roe-v -wade/.

13. Li Zhou and Youyou Zhou, "Who overturning Roe hurts most, explained in 7 charts," *Vox*, July 1, 2022, https://www.vox .com/2022/7/1/23180626/roe-dobbs-charts-impact-abortion-women -rights.

14. Casey Blake, "Alito's America: Where 'eminent' jurists believe in witches but women are the hysterics," *USA Today*, July 2, 2022,

https://www.usatoday.com/story/opinion/voices/2022/07/02/supreme
-court-abortion-alito-witches/7747134001/.

15. Alexandria Ocasio-Cortez, June 24, 2022, https://twitter.com/
AOC/status/1540354815477293056?.

16. Sean Salai, "Study finds Texas births up, abortions down after
fetal heartbeat law," *The Washington Times*, November 15, 2022, https://
www.washingtontimes.com/news/2022/nov/15/study-finds-texas
-births-abortions-down-after-feta/.

17. Ibid.

18. Dr. Michael New, "Unnoticed Victories," *Day 41*, Winter
2022–23.

19. William Cummings, "Feinstein mistakenly says 200,000 to
1,200,000 women died in illegal abortions decades ago," *USA Today*,
September 5, 2018, https://www.usatoday.com/story/news/politics/
onpolitics/2018/09/05/kavanaugh-confirmation-feinstein-illegal
-abortion-number/1206409002/.

20. Glenn Kessler, "Planned Parenthood's false stat: 'Thousands'
of women died every year before Roe, *The Washington Post*, May 29,
2019, https://www.washingtonpost.com/politics/2019/05/29/planned
-parenthoods-false-stat-thousands-women-died-every-year-before-roe/.

21. Ibid.

22. Ibid.

23. "The Pro-Life Reply to: 'Women Will Die from Illegal
Abortions," Live Action, June 25, 2019, https://www.youtube.com/watch
?v=B1s9WOBihWU&t=89s.

24. Olivia Gans and Mary Spaulding Balch, J.D., "If abortion
is made illegal women will die in back alleys," *Catholic News Agency*,
reprinted from National Right to Life, July 8, 1998, https://www
.catholicnewsagency.com/resource/55886/if-abortion-is-made-illegal
-women-will-die-in-back-alleys.

25. Lydia O'Connor, "5 Women Denied Lifesaving Abortions
Sue Texas Over Its 6-Week Ban," *HuffPost*, May 7, 2023, https://www.
huffpost.com/entry/texas-abortion-ban-lawsuit-filed_n_64077f04e4b0
e0a15960b068.

26. Kate Scanlon, "Pro-life leaders defend Texas abortion law
facing new lawsuit," *Detroit Catholic*, March 9, 2023, https://www
.detroitcatholic.com/news/pro-life-leaders-defend-texas-abortion-law
-facing-new-lawsuit.

27. Fr. Tadeusz Pacholczyk, "The care of pregnant women in Catholic hospitals," January 23, 2014, https://denvercatholic.org/care-pregnant-women-catholic-hospitals/.

28. *Catholic Online*, "Pro-life doctors: Despite Ohio bill, there is no procedure to save ectopic pregnancies," https://www.catholic.org/news/national/story.php?id=81099.

29. Matthew A.C. Newsome, "Abortion and Double Effect," *Catholic Answers*, September 1, 2006, https://www.catholic.com/magazine/print-edition/abortion-and-double-effect.

30. Students for Life of America, "Women Killed by Legal Abortion," https://studentsforlife.org/learn/women-killed-by-legal-abortion/.

31. Christine Condon, Hannah Gaskill, Jeff Barker, and Meredith Cohn, "With Roe v. Wade overturned, those seeking abortion will turn to Maryland," *The Baltimore Sun*, published June 24, 2022, updated June 25, 2022, https://www.baltimoresun.com/health/bs-hs-maryland-after-roe-v-wade-20220624-ahe4vzvoqzhitdt42imimwj5cq-story.html.

32. Korin Miller, "Explaining Jessa Duggar Seewald's spontaneous abortion and dilation and curettage procedure," *Yahoo! Life*, February 28, 2023, https://www.yahoo.com/lifestyle/jessa-duggar-seewald-spontaneous-abortion-003105624.html.

33. Virginia Allen, Lauren Evans, Kristen Eichamer, "What Pro-Abortion Activists Got Wrong About Jessa Duggar's D&C After Miscarriage," *The Daily Signal*, March 2, 2023, https://www.dailysignal.com/2023/03/02/what-pro-abortion-activists-got-wrong-about-jessa-duggars-dc-after-miscarriage/.

34. Kelsi Karruli, "A family filled with tragedy: As Jessa Duggar reveals she had to undergo a life-saving abortion after miscarriage, FEMAIL lays bare the many devastating pregnancy losses her siblings AND parents have faced," *The Daily Mail*, March 5, 2023, https://www.dailymail.co.uk/femail/article-11799329/FEMAIL-lays-bare-Duggars-devastating-pregnancies-tragedies.html.

35. Caitlin Cruz, "Jessa Duggar Seewald Had an Abortion, Even If She Won't Say the Word," *Jezebel*, February 27, 2023, https://jezebel.com/jessa-duggar-seewald-had-an-abortion-even-if-she-wont-1850163908.

36. Emily Bloch, "Jessa Duggar Seewald's pregnancy loss is bringing the abortion access conversation to the forefront," *The Philadelphia Inquirer*, February 27, 2023, https://www.inquirer.com/news/jessa-duggar-seewald-abortion-miscarriage-pregnancy-arkansas-20230227.html.

37. Allen, Evans, Eichamer, "What Pro-Abortion Activists Got Wrong About Jessa Duggar's D&C After Miscarriage."

38. Korin Miller, "Explaining Jessa Duggar Seewald's spontaneous abortion and dilation and curettage procedure."

39. John McCormack, "Jessa Duggar Seewald Had a Miscarriage, Not an Abortion," *National Review*, February 28, 2023, https://www.nationalreview.com/2023/02/jessa-duggar-seewald-had-a-miscarriage-not-an-abortion/.

Chapter 13

1. https://www.azquotes.com/author/490-Thomas_Aquinas#google_vignette.

2. Maryland Coalition Against Sexual Assault, "Rape Survivors Need Abortion Access," June 24, 2022, https://mcasa.org/news/post/rape-survivors-need-abortion-access.

3. Alia E. Dastagir, "Rape and incest account for hardly any abortions. So why are they now a focus?" *USA Today*, May 24, 2019, https://eu.usatoday.com/story/news/nation/2019/05/24/rape-and-incest-account-few-abortions-so-why-all-attention/1211175001/.

About the Authors

Shawn Carney is the cofounder, CEO, and president of 40 Days for Life and one of the most soughafter pro-life speakers today. He began as a volunteer in the pro-life movement while still in college. During this time, he helped to lead the first-ever local 40 Days for Life campaign before helping it grow to now 1,700 cities in 65 countries.

In 2019, Shawn and his wife, Marilisa, were portrayed in a major motion picture, *Unplanned*, for their role in helping a former Planned Parenthood director, Abby Johnson, during her conversion. Abby was the 26th out of more than 256 abortion workers to date who have reached out to 40 Days for Life.

Shawn is a regular media spokesperson, and his work has been featured on hundreds of outlets including NBC News, Fox News, *Fox & Friends*, the *Glenn Beck Program*, the *Laura Ingraham Show*, BBC, the *Guardian, USA Today*, CNN, and MSNBC and Christian media including the *Christian Post*,

National Catholic Register, Sirius XM Catholic Radio, EWTN Radio, and Focus on the Family.

Shawn has addressed audiences coast to coast and internationally. He has produced and hosted award-winning pro-life documentaries and is the host of the weekly *40 Days for Life* podcast. He is the coauthor of *40 Days for Life* and *What to Say When* and author of the national bestsellers *The Beginning of the End of Abortion* and *To the Heart of the Matter.* He is a member of the Knights of Columbus and the Equestrian Order of the Holy Sepulchre of Jerusalem. Shawn lives in Texas with his wife and eight children.

Steve Karlen is the campaign director at 40 Days for Life. After Steve helped lead a statewide coalition that prevented the University of Wisconsin Hospital and Clinics from opening a late-term abortion facility near the campus of his alma mater, Steve was asked to serve on the 40 Days for Life  headquarters team. In this role, Steve has helped spread the 40 Days for Life mission across the United States, Canada, and Mexico.

Steve is the editor of *Day 41* magazine, the cohost of the *40 Days for Life* podcast, and a coauthor of *What to Say When.* He has spoken in all 50 states, four Canadian provinces, and Mexico City. Steve and his work have been featured on American Family Radio, EWTN, the Christian Broadcasting Network, NBC, CBS, and Fox affiliates, as well as numerous newspapers and radio stations.

Steve lives in Madison, Wisconsin, with his wife Laura and their five children.

40 DAYS FOR LIFE.

Now that you know what to say when . . . be part of the beginning of the end of abortion!

PRAY MORE!

Find your closest 40 Days for Life vigil today:

40daysforlife.com/locations

READ MORE!

Keep up with saved lives, abortion worker conversions, and the pulse of the pro-life movement by receiving *DAY 41* quarterly magazine for FREE! Sign up at

40daysforlife.com/magazine

LISTEN MORE!

Download the weekly *40 Days for Life Podcast* for free. Guests include Peter Kreeft, Eric Metaxas, Dr. Scott Hahn, Fr. Paul Scalia, Benjamin Watson, Lila Rose, former abortion workers, and many more. Listen on any podcast app, the 40 Days for Life app, or at

40daysforlife.com/podcast

Get exclusive discounts on signed copies of this book, the first *What to Say When*, and the national bestsellers written by Shawn Carney including *The Beginning of the End of Abortion*, *To the Heart of the Matter*, and Steve Karlen's *This Is When We Begin to Fight* at 40daysforlifegear.com

Invite Shawn Carney or Steve Karlen to speak at your event by emailing **media@40daysforlife.com**.

Find out more at 40daysforlife.com